SKIING

CROWOOD SPORTS GUIDES

SKIING

TECHNIQUE•TACTICS•TRAINING

Fred Foxon

Photographs by Jean-Christophe Souillac

The Crowood Press

First published in 1991 by
The Crowood Press Ltd
Ramsbury, Marlborough
Wiltshire SN8 2HR

www.crowood.com

This impression 2005

British Library Cataloguing in Publication Data

Foxon, Fred
  Skiing: technique, tactics, training.
  1. Skiing
  I. Title
  796.93

ISBN 1 85223 571 3

Dedication

To the memory of my father.

Typeset by Chippendale Type Ltd., Otley, West Yorkshire.
Printed in Singapore by Craft Print International Ltd.

CONTENTS

ACKNOWLEDGEMENTS

Writing these acknowledgements has been a salutary reminder of the importance of the collective to the individual. Few of the ideas which follow are truly original – most have been borrowed, stolen or unconsciously absorbed. To all those ski-teachers and coaches who recognize something of theirs within these pages, I owe a broad debt of gratitude.

While these widespread sources are far too many to enumerate, there are others who have played an especially significant role. In particular, thanks to Colin Whiteside, who gave me my first teaching job and coached me through my first (and many subsequent) blunders; to John Shedden who, in addition to teaching many of us most of what we know about skiing, gave invaluable comments on parts of the manuscript; to Lesley Forrest, for her wide-ranging inspiration, ideas and suggestions; and to Martyn Hurn, for passing the project to me in the first place (thanks, Mart – now I know why you did it!).

Finally, and by no means least, to Chris Souillac of Top Ski, Val d'Isère for his patience, dedication and enthusiasm. Without his skill as both skier and photographer, the illustrations in this book would have been much the poorer. But for his encouragement, I would never have climbed back up the hill all those times to ski the shots.

Fig 1   Coming out of the sun.

PREFACE

While this book is about the nuts and bolts of skiing – its movements and techniques – that is only a means to a much more important end. Skiing is essentially about enjoyment: an escape from work, mortgage or exams; a total immersion in the cutting edge of the present, focused on the sensation of skis on snow, the rhythm of turning, the mountain views. One of its great strengths as a recreation is that it offers so many different sources of satisfaction: in learning new forms of movement, in overcoming fear, and in the achievement of personal challenge.

Even people to whom 'sport' seldom appeals can find great pleasure in skiing. In some ways, skiing has more in common with dance than with many other sports. They both share a strong sensual element, an inner aesthetic of movement, motion and rhythm. Then there is the exhilaration of controlling your adrenalin level with the challenge of each descent. The source of power is gravity – a 6,000 million million million ton motor – and apart from the price of a lift ticket it all comes for free.

For me, however, one of skiing's greatest and most enduring pleasures is that the mountains in winter are among the most beautiful places on Earth. From gentle Alpine meadows sheltered by snow-decked trees to the austere, deadly beauty of the high peaks. Just being there can be enough; to have it as a workplace is a gift.

Fig 2   Wayne Watson on the north face of the Grand Motte glacier above Tignes.

INTRODUCTION

Are Ski Books Any Use?

When writing about skiing, I sometimes get the absurd image of someone hurtling downhill trying frantically to find the page that tells them how to stop. Although this may seem a strange place to say it, I don't believe that skiing can be learned from books. But before you put it back on the shelf, I should add that I *do* believe that books play an important supporting role.

There's no substitute for a patient and sympathetic teacher, but sometimes they're hard to find. Even then, they only form half of the equation. The other half is what you bring to the learning process yourself. That includes your existing aptitudes and abilities, and an awareness of where your strengths and limitations lie; your understanding of what you want and of how you are going to achieve it; and your physical and mental preparation. The purpose of this book is to support your side of the equation. It does so on three different levels: the practical, the theoretical and the inspirational.

Firstly it gives practical exercises to try both on and off the slopes. While you can work through many of these on your own, everyone also needs the guidance of an instructor or coach. That applies as much to world-class racers as it does to recreational skiers. The exercises are intended to supplement rather than replace what you do in class.

When you are on the slopes, the most valuable activity is *doing* rather than thinking or talking. The book's second aim is, therefore, to provide explanations – to help you understand how skiing works; how the various aspects relate to each other; where you are and where you're going. This is better dealt with when sitting indoors rather than standing out on a mountain.

The third aim concerns motivation, that is your enthusiasm for the activity, your desire to learn and improve. While this may be the hardest part to deal with, I hope that something in these pages catches your imagination and convinces you that you *have* got the ability to do it, and that some of the pictures, ideas or descriptions make you want to go and give it a try.

How to Use the Book

We all have preferred styles or modes of learning: 'thinkers' need to understand the theory; 'watchers' work best from demonstrations and visual images; 'feelers' respond to the sensations of an action; and 'doers' learn by giving it a try. There tends to be a bit of each in everyone, but it helps if you recognize which is your most effective or dominant mode. Throughout the book I've tried to cater for these different styles, by giving explanations of how an action works, with descriptions of what it feels like, and images and analogies to convey the action's form. In addition, the photographs illustrate the actions in practice, giving flesh to the words on the page.

Not only are there different learning styles, but equally there are different styles of teaching. Your response to a given approach is highly individual, so it pays to be critical and selective, to find what works best for you. What follows is, therefore, meant to be used selectively. Pick the explanations, descriptions or images that strike a chord, and skip the ones that don't make sense. There's no point in getting hung up with things that don't work; rather, aim to focus on the positive, the ones that do work, and build on those.

PART I
TRAINING AND PREPARATION

CHAPTER I

LEARNING TO SKI

Skiing is usually thought of in terms of technique. Snowplough, basic swing and parallel turns; traversing, side-slipping and skidding – these are the elements which must be learned. And yet the movements involved in these manoeuvres are actually very simple. Compared with playing a piano, they're trivial.

Not only are the movements themselves fairly simple, they're also similar to ones that non-skiers already use. Watch a skier making a turn. Whether parallel or in a plough, the outer leg of the turn does much the same thing, i.e. bending to put pressure on the ski and moving the thigh inwards to edge it. The action is almost identical to that of runners making a swerve: in preparation to push off into the new direction, they sink down onto the outer foot; at the same time, the knee and hip move across into the direction of the

swerve. In fact, the movements in skiing are even simpler. While runners must extend their leg to propel themselves into the new direction, skiers need only keep the leg flexed to carry them round the turn.

Even the basic posture of skiing is similar to that of other active, dynamic sports. The flexed, 'ready for action' body shape is like that of a tennis player waiting to receive a service, or a goalkeeper facing a penalty.

In a sense, even complete novices already know how to perform many of the movements involved in skiing. They're part of the repertoire we all possess as human beings. Our repertoire originates in the games and activities of childhood: running, tumbling, climbing, catching, chasing, dodging. Even if as adults we're stiffer and slower, we still know how to do

these things. We 'know' in the sense of knowing how to ride a bike, which doesn't necessarily mean understanding the physics of it.

Movement and the Body Management System

Human beings have a very sophisticated 'body management system', which operates at various different levels. Some functions are completely automatic, for example, co-ordinating the muscles to swallow and digest a piece of food, and to disperse the nutrients through the body. There are others which normally operate without conscious control, but can be monitored and influenced if necessary. Try the following example:

Fig 3 (a) and (b)   A comparison of plough and parallel turns. In both manoeuvres, the skier's outer (right) leg and body profile are identical. Only the position of the inside leg and ski are different.

(a)

(b)

Get up and stand on one leg. Feel the myriad tiny movements in that leg and foot – and indeed elsewhere in your body – as you maintain your balance.

These movements of balancing are used every day, for getting out of a chair, reaching a high shelf, walking across the room. We normally don't give them a second thought, and yet they involve immensely complex and precise feats of co-ordination. Without them, you couldn't even stand upright.

I have heard people say, 'Oh, I wouldn't be any good at skiing – I don't have very good balance'. That same person might be seen weaving their way down a crowded office staircase carrying a stack of files, while wearing 3in heels. If that isn't good balance, I don't know what is. In skiing the main difference is that what you are standing on is itself in motion. In effect you're balancing on a moving platform. A better analogy would be that of walking down the corridor of a moving train. Of

Fig 4   A runner's swerve. Compare the runner's body profile with that of the skier.

Fig 5   A goalkeeper, tennis player and skier. All three use the same basic 'ready for action' stance.

course, you might not make it without the occasional stumble; but even the best skiers in the world do not *always* stay on their feet.

Our conscious actions are generally at a much higher level, for example, choosing which shops to visit or deciding to make a cup of coffee. Most of the actual movements – walking, picking things up, swallowing – are automatic.

This is not to say that movements don't have to be learned, or that they always operate unconsciously. When learning to drive a car, the actions of depressing and releasing the clutch or throttle are in themselves extremely simple, but co-ordinating them when changing gear takes practice and attention.

In learning to ski, two processes are involved. First is discovering which movements to use out of a repertoire which we already know how to perform. In the main these are fairly simple movements of the legs and feet, involving bending, straightening, tilting and turning. Second is the matter of putting them together in new sequences and combinations. Here, the task is learning to co-ordinate already-known movements, just like learning to use the throttle and clutch in synchrony.

In other words, learning the movements of skiing is less about learning *how* to make these movements, and more a matter of finding out which ones to use. Having made that discovery, it involves learning to co-ordinate their sequence and timing. Even complete novices have enormous resources to draw on. Their highly sophisticated body management system is capable of balancing in all sorts of situations, and has a huge vocabulary of movement, out of which the required sequences of action can be built.

Co-ordination and timing must be consciously developed, but below the conscious level, a huge range of processes operate in the background. Like the pilot of a modern computerized aircraft, you only need attend to the overall task, while these other processes work automatically in support.

Movement and Co-ordination

Co-ordination is a key factor. Good skiers link their movements together into an integrated whole so that they blend and merge, rather than performing a disjointed succession of separate movements. That's true of virtually all skilled movement. Although you can describe the action of walking in terms of separate strides, people don't actually move like 1950s' sci-fi robots. There's no clear break where one movement ends and the next begins.

When first learning a new activity, you learn individual parts, then put them together. At first they don't link very well, but then gradually they merge and flow. This aspect of the learning process is essentially one of integration – linking together larger and larger sequences into higher-order actions. It can be likened to learning a new piece on a musical instrument. At first you can only link one or two notes together; later, a whole phrase or passage becomes combined. Your awareness alters too. It moves from focusing on the next note to be played, to the next phrase, to higher-order features

still, such as the relative timing and intensity of successive phrases.

This process of integration is one which it's important to foster. Rather than trying to hone each component to perfection before combining them, it's best to have a go at the whole thing at an early stage. A 'whole – part' approach is often more effective than a 'part – whole' one. That is, to start with the whole action in rough form, and refine the constituent parts later, rather than learning all the elements before combining them.

After all, skiing isn't a matter of doing perfect turns. It's a form of locomotion that lets you move around in a strange and sometimes hostile environment, to explore and enjoy the natural world. At the very earliest stages, you can appreciate the beauty of the mountains, even if the locomotion itself doesn't feel so good!

Indeed, for many people, impeccable technique may be neither desirable nor feasible. Enjoyment may be found in having the bare minimum of technique necessary to get around the mountains in winter. Even when your aim is for improved technique, remember that the broader picture is important too. Turns work

Fig 6   Skiing isn't just about making perfect turns – it's a way of exploring an alien and beautiful environment.

better when they're linked, and skiing feels more effortless when your actions have rhythm and flow.

Movement and Feedback

To achieve co-ordination, you need to be aware of the results of your own actions. Rather than your brain always telling your body what to do, you need to tune into your body and feel what it is telling your brain. The movements of skiing are adjusted according to the terrain, as well as being co-ordinated with each other, and have specific effects on the skis' behaviour. In order to judge their timing and intensity, you must be sensitive to feedback, from both the outside world and from within your own body.

That feedback comes from many sources. Of the five senses, taste and smell don't play a very large part, except at lunchtime, but there is a sixth one which has a very significant role. That is, your kinaesthetic sense or body awareness – the ability to feel what your body is doing without having to look. It tells you which way up you are, where your feet are in relation to each other, how fast you are moving, and so on. But you need to tune in to it and develop your sensitivity. Learning to ski does not just involve learning to do; it means learning to see and feel as well, i.e. reading the terrain, choosing a line, monitoring the response of the skis. As skill improves, the accuracy of both movement and awareness must increase.

Words and Images

Words are sometimes very clumsy tools for communicating movement. Try the following exercise:

Have a friend lie on the floor, then tell them how to get up. Don't just say 'Get up!', but describe the individual movements which should be made. Their task is to follow your instructions blindly to the letter.

This gives an amusing illustration of how poorly we can convey the details of a simple action (like getting up) by way of a description (like 'Bend your left leg to bring your heel close to your bottom, slide your left hand back to bring it underneath your shoulder . . .' etc.).

To put it another way, your body does not speak English. What it does understand is how to do a huge variety of complex actions like getting up off the floor, catching a ball, running and jumping.

STAR TIP

Verbal instructions may provide us with a great many facts about skiing. The problem is how to convert these complex concepts into actions! Our bodies do not understand English, French or Italian, so the verbal instructions that we bombard ourselves with are falling on deaf ears.
                                    Sarah Ferguson
                        Skiing from the Inside, 1989

One of the easiest ways to tap into that repertoire is by way of image and analogy. In terms of the actions of skiing, these might be: 'Imagine you're a tennis player waiting for service'; 'Stand as if you're preparing to spring off your left foot'; or 'Imagine you're pedalling a bicycle as you press down on alternate skis'. Images can also be used to improve your awareness. For example, imagining you are balancing a book on your head can help you discover how effectively your legs absorb bumps in the terrain.

Pictures and Actions

The saying, 'A picture's worth a thousand words' is nowhere more true than in learning to ski. The picture in question can be one that is evoked through words, like the images above, or one that is shown directly. The latter might be a demonstration or a film replay. Watching film and video can be a very effective learning aid. Even an instructor whose English is not very good can still demonstrate what is required. However, the way in which you view it influences its effectiveness.

Children are very good imitators. Even young babies quickly learn to recognize and imitate facial gestures like smiling or sticking out their tongue. But in adulthood, that ability often falls into disuse. We don't so much lose it as learn to interpret what we see in other ways. Instead of just imitating, we learn to analyse the meaning behind the gesture – the 'how' and 'why' of what's being done. Analysing what we see is an extremely important ability; it lies at the very heart of both art and science, but it often inhibits the performance of physical tasks. In a nutshell, analysis leads to paralysis:

Say the words 'water chestnut', and try to analyse the action. Feel the movements of your tongue, lips, teeth, jaws and throat. It's remarkably complex, and you have to say the words impossibly slowly to make out what's going on. Here, analysis interferes with performance.

In skiing too, analysis can be counter-productive. When you watch a demonstration, you can look at it in one of two ways. Either to dissect it and understand how it works, or to see it as a whole – a single integrated action to be imitated. As a basis for performance, the second is much more effective. That's not to deny the value of understanding, but it has a more indirect, supporting role.

The instructor's description of the task can be used in either of the same two ways – as an analysis of the movements, or to draw attention to the key features of the manoeuvre:

'As you plant your ski pole, make an up-movement and start to turn your legs and feet. As the skis reach the fall-line, begin sinking down again and continue turning your feet. As your skis turn further from the fall-line, press your knees and hips across into the hill.'

Rather than trying to 'ski by numbers' – . . . 'first plant my pole . . . then straighten my legs . . . now turn my feet . . .' – it's much

Fig 7 (a)–(d)   Image and Action.

(b)

(a)

Fig 7 (a)–(d)   During a demonstration, imagine yourself performing the action as you watch. Then when you set out to do it yourself, aim to re-create that imaginary performance.

(c)

(d)

better to have a picture in your mind's eye and aim to copy it. The words simply bring the key features into sharper relief.

Image and Imagination

You can also go beyond the picture itself. When watching a demonstration, use your imagination to 'get inside' the instructor's body. Imagine what the movements feel like as you look. As you visualize yourself performing the action, imagine how it feels. Then when you set off to do it for real, aim to re-create that entire image, both appearance and sensation.

Mental imaging or visualization is very useful not only for learning new techniques, but also to maintain performance in difficult conditions. It's a key element in the training of top athletes, but has just as much value for beginners and recreational performers.

The competitor can mentally rehearse an image of their optimum performance. The rehearsal also helps filter out the interferences, i.e. spectators, other competitors, the sense of occasion, the pressure. In the same way, when standing nervously at the top of a difficult run, looking down it doesn't help. Instead, close your eyes and imagine yourself confidently skiing the run. Once you have established a strong model for your actions, set off and do it for real.

Perception and Performance

One of the difficulties faced by inexperienced skiers is learning to interpret their surroundings. Unlike our everyday world of buildings, trees and roads, the mountains in winter are a very stark and sparse environment. Above the tree-line, the snow-fields are a featureless white desert of soft, diffuse contours. Even in good visibility, the terrain contains little colour or contrast, few clearly defined boundaries or shapes. Overcast or misty conditions make it even harder to see. At the extreme is what's called a 'white-out', when you're within a layer of low cloud, so that snow merges with sky. Your horizon and other points of reference disappear,

Fig 8 (a) Learning to see is just as important as learning to ski. The high mountains are an environment of diffuse contours and limited visual detail. In cloudy weather, it's even harder to make out the features of the terrain.

leaving you lost inside a floodlit ping-pong ball.

Learning to see in such an environment is just as important as learning to ski. Your eyes must become attuned to the subtle cues that reveal the terrain: the faint shading which indicates a bump, the brownish tinge of old, polished ice; the matt appearance of wind-packed snow. Other senses also provide useful information. The sound of your skis gives clues about the snow's hardness and texture; and the sensations through your legs and feet give you feedback about the skis' response.

Focused Attention

To pick up that information, you have to focus on it. Your attention is like a spotlight in a darkened room. Rather than letting it be drawn hither and thither at random, aim it on what you want to see. It can be 'focused' into a wide beam, or into a narrow pencil of light. A wide-angle view helps you choose your route, but when skiing down a tricky section, you must home in on a small shifting area, to pick your line and find the easiest places to turn.

Sometimes your attention gets aimed in the wrong direction altogether. In bad

Once you're moving, a wide focus often gives too much information and can create distractions and anxiety.

A narrow focus helps you pick your line down the mountain and choose the best places to turn.

Fig 8 (b) In wide-angle, you're able to pick up a wealth of detail. It enables you to enjoy the view, work out where you are or locate a friend. However, once in motion, you need a narrow 'spotlight' to pick your line down the mountain.

visibility, trying too hard to see the terrain simply blocks out the other senses – the sound of the skis, the feel of their response. While you need to keep looking, you must tune in to your other senses too.

The importance of focus applies to your actions as well as your perception. If you consciously try to do two things at once, neither one works well. Even if they normally operate in unison, you can only really pay attention to one at a time. That is why it's better to have an image of the overall pattern, rather than a procedure or a list of instructions to follow. The image lets you develop the whole action in rough form, which you can then refine by focusing on individual elements one by one.

you with the best possible means of evaluating their effectiveness, and consequently of discovering the optimum amount of change.

Self-Trust

It's easy to put all the responsibility for the learning process on your instructor, but all they can do is help you along the way. It's *your* body which learns to ski, and *your* senses which tell you what is going on. To evaluate your actions, you must not only be aware of their consequences, but also trust the information you receive. You first

must trust yourself to go ahead and do it, then trust the validity of the feedback that arises.

That's not to say that you're not sometimes mistaken. Your movements often feel much bigger than they really are. Even after being told to exaggerate them, it's hard to believe they are not as big as is physically possible.

Sometimes your awareness of movement must be re-calibrated. When learning a new action, your body automatically restricts its range of movement. If you're feeling nervous, the effect is magnified by muscle-tension.

Raising Awareness

Instructors often give commands like 'Bend your ankles! Face downhill! Don't stick your bottom out!' They all seem very simple and straightforward, and yet they can be quite hard to put into practice.

Part of the difficulty is lack of awareness of what you're currently doing. If you don't know where you are right now, it's very difficult to get where you want to be. That's as true of altering your actions as it is of navigating with a map. Knowing where on the map you are aiming for is not much use unless you also know your present location. Therefore, to start with, turn the command into a question: 'How much are my ankles bending? Which way is my body facing? What am I doing with my bottom?' Answering these questions raises your awareness of your current actions, making it easier to effect the desired changes. With greater sensitivity to your actions, you can more accurately judge how much change to make.

Skiers often get blocked by 'rules'. Commands like 'Keep your weight forward' become enshrined into rules which must not be broken, but their intended purpose was much more limited – to correct a fault at a particular moment. If you're in tune with the feedback from your skis and body, you can feel the effects of modifying your actions. That provides

Fig 9 (a) and (b)   When learning something new, you may feel as if you're moving as much as in (a), when in fact your movements are more like those in (b).

Once again, tuning in to your body is the most effective remedy. By finding where the tension is, you can ease it away. By comparing the extent of your movements while standing still with those when skiing, you can discover the restrictions that exist.

Video Feedback

One of the most powerful ways of improving your awareness is by seeing yourself on video. However, it can also be a very destructive experience. While the camera may never lie, it also seldom flatters. It's made worse by the fact that we're often our own worst critics. You can think of it as the 'bathroom mirror syndrome' – the fact that we are seldom completely satisfied with our own appearance.

In addition, skiing is a highly visual activity. It appeals to the show-off in everyone – at least, if charging about in brightly coloured clothing against a brilliant white backdrop can be called exhibitionism. Therefore, when precious self-images are shattered, the effect can be anything but positive. For that reason, video is a tool which must be used with care. However, if the aim is improved body awareness, you must get used to seeing what you're really doing.

The first time you see yourself on screen it can come as rather a shock. When you felt like a World Cup racer gracefully swooping at breathtaking speed down an impossibly steep hillside, it's hard to identify with the ungainly figure slowly lurching down a barely perceptible slope. That's not to deny the validity of the exhilaration which you experienced; at all levels of performance, it's one of skiing's greatest joys.

Before you can use video constructively, you must overcome the emotional distractions and start seeing yourself objectively – to move beyond the initial reaction of 'Oh God, that isn't really me is it?' First, simply watch it through a few times and get used to your appearance. Don't try to analyse it, just aim for a balanced impression, seeing your strengths as well as your weaknesses.

Fig 10   If you felt like this, you may be disappointed when you see the video replay!

Next, relate what you see with your memory of how it felt. The aim is to improve the accuracy of your body-image – the match between what you felt you were doing and the reality of your actual movements. The result is a clearer, more accurate model for the future. Not so much a list of commands or instructions – 'Hold my hands lower' or 'Stand taller' – rather, a picture of how the action should look and an image of how it should feel.

The Fear Factor

One of the greatest impediments to effective performance is fear. It makes your actions tentative and your body tense, so that movements that were smooth become jerky. Most destructive of all, the activity stops being fun. However, fear is only an extension of excitement, like the mutual proximity of laughter and tears. One of skiing's greatest sources of enjoyment is the exhilaration – of speed and steepness, the wind in your face, the danger and daring.

The trick is keeping it at an appropriate level: too little, and the activity becomes dull; too much, and exhilaration becomes anxiety and fear. A good starting point is to recognize your emotional reactions and monitor where you are on the 'arousal curve' (as shown in Fig 11 on page 20). The relationship between your ability to ski and your level of excitement or fear can neatly be described in terms of this curve.

If you're bored or sleepy, you don't perform anywhere near your best. As your level of arousal rises through alertness and exhilaration, performance also improves. That continues to a peak, beyond which exhilaration turns into anxiety. It's aptly described as 'going over the top'. In competition, for example, if an athlete becomes over-excited their performance falls apart.

The trouble is that the process is not always reversible. Sometimes it reaches such a pitch that everything collapses – your heart races, your mind goes blank, you freeze up and can't even move. At that point, it's no good just easing the pressure a little bit; sometimes you have to get away from the situation completely before you can recover. In other words, someone who has just panicked on a steep

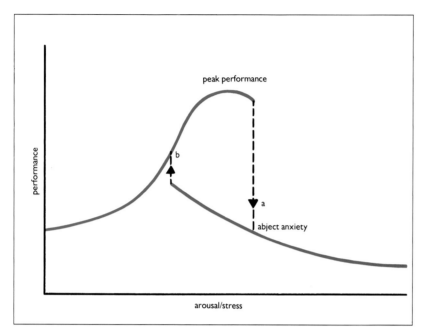

Fig 11   When you're bored or tired, performance is poor. As the level of interest and excitement rises, performance also improves; but beyond the peak, exhilaration turns into anxiety and panic. With increasing arousal, performance follows route A; but following a collapse of confidence, the return is by the lower pathway B.

red run may still be tense and nervous on a moderate blue. They may need a spell on gentle greens before regaining their composure, or even half an hour in a mountain cafe. In Fig 11, the route into panic is by A; the return to confidence and composure follows B.

It's no help being dragged around the mountains by much stronger or more confident skiers. For progress and enjoyment, you need terrain that is within your 'comfort zone'. That's not to deny the importance of challenge, but it must be appropriate to both your technical ability and your confidence.

Anxiety and Action

Anxiety has several effects on your actions: it causes muscle tension, interfering with mobility and balance, and it leads to inappropriate movements and posture, restricting your control. Many of these changes are consistent and

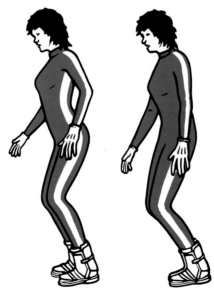

Fig 12   The 'goalkeeper' position versus the 'Eek!' position.

predictable. Your toes clench, pushing you back on your heels, and your shoulders and spine tense up, straightening your body and hollowing your lower back. The resulting body shape can be described as the 'Eek!' position, compared with a relaxed and confident 'goalkeeper' stance.

Many skiers acquire the 'Eek!' posture early in their learning. Through poor instruction or spending too much time on difficult runs, it becomes habitual even when they're not actually scared. Muscle tension makes your movements jerky, interfering with balance and control. It cuts down your awareness of feedback, restricting your capacity to respond and learn.

Coping with Fear

For complete beginners, the environment itself is so unfamiliar that it can create anxiety. For experienced skiers, even terrain that's well within their technical ability can sometimes look frightening. For example, many intermediate runs follow tracks which are cut across the mountain. The downhill side often has a blind lip, giving the appearance of a hidden abyss. Long slopes look steeper than short ones, because it's further to the bottom. Crowded runs look more difficult than quiet ones, with more distractions and obstacles to avoid. Even very experienced skiers find convex slopes intimidating. Where the terrain drops away out of sight, it looks much steeper and more dangerous than it often is.

In these situations, focused attention is often the best remedy. Instead of taking in the wide-angle view – seeing how steep, long, busy, bumpy and icy the run is – just focus on where your first turn is going to be:

Keep your spotlight on the immediate situation. To filter out the distractions and fear-provoking features, concentrate on identifying the snow texture, reading the terrain, choosing your line.

Focusing on the source of your fear can also help. The blind drop-off at the edge of a run may only be a gentle bank, but as long as it remains hidden, it possesses imaginary dangers. One of the strongest

Fig 13 Runs like this can be intimidating because the terrain drops away out of sight.

sources of fear is the unknown. By taking a closer look, many such fears evaporate.

To deal with muscle tension, you must learn to relax. Practise indoors in comfortable, familiar surroundings. Start by focusing on your breathing; if it's deep and slow, your body automatically relaxes more than when it's fast and shallow:

Let your head flop forwards and your arms hang down. With each out-breath, feel the tension draining from your muscles. Imagine water flowing through your limbs, dissolving the stiffness away. Work through your whole body, releasing the tension as you go. Start at your toes and work up to your neck and head.

Before tackling an intimidating run, spend a

moment on that routine. Then, with your breathing slow and your body loose, set off. Monitor your breathing as you ski, maintaining a slow, steady rhythm. You can also link your breathing to your turns. By breathing in as you start each turn and out as you finish, it helps keep your movements smooth and relaxed.

Another method which has already been mentioned is visualization. By closing your eyes and imagining yourself skiing confidently, you can create a model for what you're about to do, and re-affirm your ability to do it. Visualization works best if it's coupled with the breathing and relaxation exercises. If you're tense and nervous, spend a moment in preparation:

1. Close your eyes and slow your

breathing. When everything is relaxed, visualize your first few turns.
2. Once you have a positive image, open your eyes and set off before any distractions return.

In themselves, relaxation and visualization also help to filter out the sources of fear. By focusing your mind, attention is switched from negative thoughts. The same is true when you are actually skiing. The activity focuses you on the task in hand – choosing a line, controlling your body and skis. If there is a difficult section ahead, keep going rather than stopping. Your attention stays focused and your rhythm helps keep your movements smooth and loose.

Individuality

In everyday life we recognize ourselves and others as individuals. We see differences in build, height and facial features; in the ways we talk and move; in age and sex. You can recognize a friend in the distance, not just by their face or clothes, but by their style of walking. Everyone has individual patterns of movement, such as their speed and style of gait. These characteristics are linked with other body features, such as height, weight, strength and shape. They are also related to personality and mood – outgoing or reserved; happy or sad.

Skiing is no different from speaking or walking. As well as having confidence in yourself, you must acknowledge your individuality. A short, stocky person does not ski like a tall, slim one. That's not to say they can't both ski gracefully and efficiently; it's just that the shape of their bodies and the pattern of their movements are distinct. That's especially true between men and women. Female skiers move differently to males.

The differences are of detail rather than overall structure. We all use the same basic movement pattern for walking – swinging two legs forward at once doesn't work very well unless you're a horse. In skiing too, we all use similar patterns of movement, but the precise form varies from person to person. It's important to recognize and accept these differences, especially when modelling your performance on someone else.

Taking Sides

One of the most deeply rooted individual features is hand preference. Only a tiny proportion of people are truly ambidextrous. That has obvious consequences in activities like tennis or golf, but in skiing, too, it has an effect.

Most right-handers also favour their right leg – when kicking a ball, for example.

The leg isn't necessarily stronger; rather, confidence and co-ordination are better on that side. It's more accurate, therefore, to think in terms of 'sidedness' than 'handedness'. As a result, most people find it easier to turn one way than the other. In snowplough, right-sided skiers usually turn better to the left, since the right ski controls that turn. Then in basic swing, it's often the right turn which is better, since now the inside leg must learn the new action.

It's important to recognize the effect on your skiing. There's no secret to becoming a symmetrical, balanced skier – it's simply a matter of practising to your less-favoured side. It's most noticeable in three situations: setting off on your first turn, stopping, and on difficult terrain. Therefore, make a point of not giving in to your preference. By setting off and stopping with your poorer turn, you'll become equally confident on both sides.

Children and Adults

Children ski differently to adults. Especially when very young, they have proportionately larger heads, giving them a higher centre of mass. Their strength or power-to-weight ratio is less, making it harder for them to move in certain ways. On the other hand, their inertia is lower, so children can often make their skis grip and turn more easily than adults.

When copying adults, children naturally adapt the actions to suit their own bodies. But sometimes they're encouraged to ski inappropriately, by trying to copy an adult's actions in detail.

That's particularly true of posture. Instead of a 'goalkeeper' stance, young children often lean their legs back against their boots, while crouching the upper body forward. It's inefficient for adults, but is appropriate for young children unless they're technically very advanced.

Shape, Size and Strength

Some skiers can do things that are quite impossible for others. A young, fit person can often get down slopes that are far beyond their technical ability, due to

confidence, strength and stamina. That's not to say it's a good way to become proficient. Less strong and confident skiers often develop better judgement and skill, even if they don't tackle such difficult terrain.

Even getting up from a fall is much easier for some people than others. For example, men generally have an advantage over women in having more powerful arms and shoulders. To compensate, women can use their often greater flexibility.

Light individuals can ski in conditions that are impossible for a heavy person. In soft or crusty snow, the heavier skier may sink too deeply to turn, while the lighter one remains nearer the surface.

People with longer legs can absorb bigger bumps. In consequence, downhill racers are often fairly tall, allowing them to cope more easily with undulations at high speed. By comparison, until the advent of flexible slalom poles ('rapid gates'), successful slalom racers were often smaller and more compact, since the quick, tight turns favoured more agile skiers. (The new poles allow racers' bodies to take a straighter line, often passing inside the gate itself. In consequence, the smaller skier's agility now gives less of an advantage.)

However, the main point is not whether you're more or less well suited to skiing, as people of all ages, types and dispositions can achieve great satisfaction and enjoyment from the sport. Rather, it's a matter of knowing yourself, of recognizing your own strengths and weaknesses, so that you can set appropriate and realistic goals.

Fig 14 Opposite: Wayne Watson in action.

Fig 15   The Grande Motte, Tignes.

Technique, Skill and Style

Individuality is often expressed in terms of personal style. It's reflected in your movement, speech and dress. While the same is true in skiing, here style also has a broader sense.

Different instructors and national ski schools place different emphases and embellishments on what they teach. While the mechanics of skiing remain the same no matter where you are, its style may vary. Some approaches are more stylized than others. Standing tall with your feet clamped together and your hands high and wide may look cool, but it's much less effective than the 'goalkeeper' stance used by racers.

On the other hand, skill is the ability to apply technique appropriately to the situation and your level of confidence. If skill is the substance of your skiing – the essential ingredients which get you down a mountain – then style is the packaging in which it's wrapped.

The emphasis in these pages is on learning efficient, effective actions, and on developing the awareness to apply them skilfully. Within that framework, there is lots of room for individual style and self-expression. Skill is what gets you down mountains; style should be a secondary embellishment, reflecting but never governing your skill.

CHAPTER 2

CLOTHING AND EQUIPMENT

When going skiing, you need the right tools for the job. Clothing and equipment that's not well maintained or appropriate for the conditions reduces enjoyment and performance, and compromises on safety.

Clothing

Ski clothing has to deal with a wide range of demands: it must protect you from the elements, keeping you warm in a blizzard, even when sitting still on a chair-lift; it must give the freedom of movement needed in an active sport; and it must allow regulation of warmth to prevent overheating when working hard.

Ski Suits

Ski suits come in both one- and two-piece designs. Each has its advantages and drawbacks. In bad weather and in deep snow, one-piece suits have fewer entry points for snow to get inside, but their main drawbacks are that the jacket can't be removed in hot weather, and they're inconvenient when going to the toilet, especially for women. In the less user-friendly establishments, keeping everything off the floor requires three arms. Two-piece suits are generally more versatile and convenient. They can also be warmer due to their overlap around the midriff. When choosing a suit, make sure it still overlaps when crouching down.

The materials from which suits are made are important. Normally, the outer is a nylon fabric. On more expensive high-tech models, this may incorporate a breathable waterproof membrane such as Gore-Tex or Entrant. These membranes

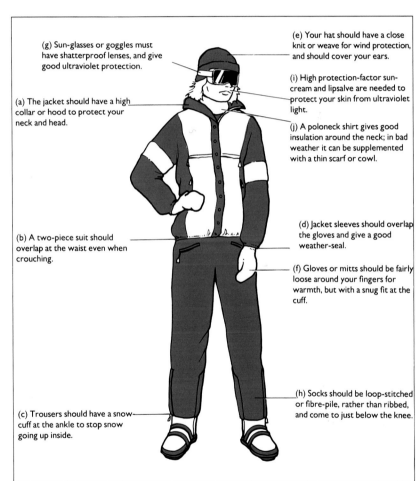

(g) Sun-glasses or goggles must have shatterproof lenses, and give good ultraviolet protection.

(a) The jacket should have a high collar or hood to protect your neck and head.

(b) A two-piece suit should overlap at the waist even when crouching.

(c) Trousers should have a snow-cuff at the ankle to stop snow going up inside.

(e) Your hat should have a close knit or weave for wind protection, and should cover your ears.

(i) High protection-factor sun-cream and lipsalve are needed to protect your skin from ultraviolet light.

(j) A poloneck shirt gives good insulation around the neck; in bad weather it can be supplemented with a thin scarf or cowl.

(d) Jacket sleeves should overlap the gloves and give a good weather-seal.

(f) Gloves or mitts should be fairly loose around your fingers for warmth, but with a snug fit at the cuff.

(h) Socks should be loop-stitched or fibre-pile, rather than ribbed, and come to just below the knee.

Fig 16   Ski clothing.

not only help keep you dry, but are also windproof. Except for lightweight shell garments, ski suits also have an insulating layer. This may be standard polyester wadding, or else one of the more efficient materials such as Thinsulate or Isodry.

When choosing a suit, several factors should be borne in mind:

● It should have a high collar or hood to protect your neck and head in bad weather.

● Adequate pockets are needed for sun-cream, sun-glasses, hat, etc. These should be zipped, as Velcro closures can clog with snow and fail to fasten securely.

● Trousers should have a snow-trap at the ankle, either an elasticated hem or a separate inner cuff, to stop snow going up the trouser leg.

● The jacket of a two-piece should overlap the trousers even when crouching. The sleeves must be long enough to overlap the gloves, with cuffs giving an effective weather seal.

● The outer fabric should be fairly windproof, and made of anti-slip material.

● A suit that's too tight compresses the insulation, reducing warmth. Unless it's made of stretch fabric, it's also more likely to tear. Make sure it allows a full range of movement.

Inner Clothing

Especially in cold weather, it's best to use thermal underwear next to your skin – a long-sleeved vest and a pair of long johns. Nylon doesn't absorb perspiration, and keeps your skin moist and clammy. Natural fibres such as wool, cotton and silk are much better, since they absorb moisture and therefore keep the skin dry. However, some synthetic fabrics such as chlorofibre and polypropylene are specially designed for the purpose. By wicking moisture from the skin towards the outer layers, they keep your skin dry in situations where natural fibres would eventually get damp.

For warmth it's best to wear several thin layers rather than one thick one. Each garment traps a layer of air, increasing the insulation. By adding or removing layers, it also allows more versatile temperature control. In cold weather you may need thermal underwear, a cotton polo neck, a shirt and a thin sweater beneath your suit.

Hats

A good hat is vital to prevent heat loss. It should cover your ears, and have a close enough knit or weave to give good wind protection. A thin scarf also helps keep your neck warm.

Gloves

Ski gloves need a tough, non-slip palm reinforcement and good insulation. For warmth, they should be fairly loose, which also leaves room for a pair of inner gloves when needed. Unless they are good quality and regularly treated with a proofing agent, leather gloves easily become waterlogged. Gloves are more convenient than mitts, but are not as warm. In either case, they need a long enough cuff not to leave a gap at your wrist, even with arms outstretched. Exposed wrists chills the blood supply to the hands.

Socks

Ski socks should have a high wool content, and should reach just below the knee. For comfort you need a loop-stitch or fibre-pile design rather than ribbing. Only one pair of socks should be worn at a time, otherwise they tend to wrinkle against each other and cause blisters.

Accessories

Eye Protection

For eye protection, you need good-quality sun-glasses or goggles. These should be a secure fit and have total ultraviolet protection, shatterproof lenses, and a design which screens glare around the edges. The amount of ultraviolet is greater at altitude than at sea-level, and is increased by reflection off snow and cloud. This radiation causes sore eyes, snow-blindness, and the longer-term risk of cataracts.

Goggles give good protection against wind and falling snow as well as radiation. To prevent problems with misting, they should have a double lens with an anti-fog coating. In sunny weather, goggles may be too hot, so sun-glasses are also needed.

Sunscreen

The high levels of ultraviolet make suncream essential. The risks are not only of sunburn, but also of solar keratosis and skin cancer in the longer term. High protection suncream (from factor 8 upwards) should be used even in early season; later, factors 20–30 or total block may be needed.

Apply it regularly, including the ear-lobes and the underside of your nose and chin. Remember that even with cloud cover, there can still be a high level of ultraviolet. To moisturize and screen your lips, use a total sunblock lipsalve.

Equipment

For your first trip it's best to hire skis and boots, but if you intend skiing regularly, a well-fitting pair of boots are a worthwhile investment even after the first few days. Skis and bindings can be left till later, at least until you can make linked turns on easy slopes and use a lift. By that stage, you can cope with an intermediate-level ski, which is a better investment than one designed for complete novices.

Ski Boots

Ski boots are the steering-linkage connecting your feet and legs to the skis. Appropriate and well-fitting boots should satisfy several criteria:

● A snug, comfortable fit with no pressure points or rubbing.

● Firm support around the instep, ankle and lower leg, to minimize movement within the boot.

● Enough space around the toes to wriggle them freely.

● A good range of forward ankle flex, but stopping before the joint reaches its limit of movement.

● Firm lateral support, so that any sideways tilting of the leg is transmitted accurately to the skis.

There are two basic designs: top entry and rear entry. All have a stiff plastic shell, and a stitched or moulded inner boot padded with foam. The final choice should always be in terms of comfort. Provided it's suitable for your build and

comfort and good arch support, foot-beds can be custom-made. For the ultimate accuracy of fit, foam-injected inners are moulded to your feet.

Ski boots should hold the ankle and instep securely without cramping your toes. Any significant movement of the foot inside the boot increases the risk of injury and reduces control. For that reason, boots must always be firmly done up when skiing.

Skis

Apart from being turned up at the front to stop them digging in, skis have two main characteristics: a base which slides easily, and metal edges which bite into the snow. These allow the skis to slide freely along their length, but to resist sideways movement when tilted on edge. However, modern skis are considerably more sophisticated than that. As well as being able to slide and grip, they are also designed to turn, due to several additional features:

● Camber. Like the human foot, skis have a natural arch which ensures that the whole length of the ski presses firmly against the snow.
● Side-cut. Skis are widest at the front, narrowest in the middle, becoming wider again towards the tail.
● Flex. Like an archer's bow, skis are softest at the extremities and stiffest in the middle. The front section is usually softer than the rear.

Due to the ski's side-cut and flex, it forms a curve rather than a straight line when its edge is pressed against the snow. As a result, the ski is naturally inclined to turn. You can demonstrate the effect indoors with a piece of stiff card cut to the shape illustrated in Fig 18(b). Tilted on edge, it runs in a curve when pressed against a carpet. If a ruler is used instead, it runs in a straight line.

In most skiing situations there's actually a degree of skid when turning, rather than the total grip illustrated with the card. However, the basic principle still applies. Skis are precision-made tools which are designed to turn.

Fig 17   Ski boots come in two designs – top- and rear-entry.

ability, there's no over-riding advantage to either type.

Rear-entry boots are popular in rental shops, since they're simpler to put on and adjust. Your foot slides in easily, and they only have one or two clips to fasten. Most beginner and intermediate boots are rear entry, but there are also some excellent high-performance models of this type. Top-entry boots are mostly designed for fairly experienced skiers. They can give a very responsive and precise fit, but are often harder to put on and take off. The larger number of clips also take longer to fasten.

Boot Fitting
Make sure your socks have no wrinkles, and that the elasticated snow-cuff on your trousers is pulled over the top of the boot rather than tucked inside. Seams or ridges within the boot cause blisters. A well-fitting boot initially feels tight. Put it on, fasten the clips, then flex your ankle forwards several times to bed your foot into it. Your toes will normally touch the end until you do this, but if they still touch after flexing forward, the boot is too small.

When buying rather than hiring, pressure points can be dealt with by a skilled boot-fitter. Ring-shaped pads can ease pressure on the ankle-bone or foot; on the shins, it can be alleviated with strips of padding down either side of the bone. On boots with a pre-moulded inner, foam can be ground away for a better fit. If the boot is too narrow, the shell can also be stretched using specialist tools. For

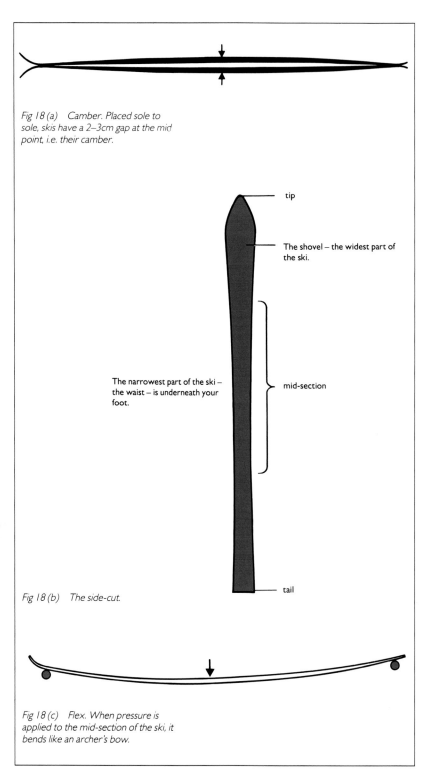

Fig 18 (a)   Camber. Placed sole to sole, skis have a 2–3cm gap at the mid point, i.e. their camber.

tip

The shovel – the widest part of the ski.

The narrowest part of the ski – the waist – is underneath your foot.

mid-section

tail

Fig 18 (b)   The side-cut.

Fig 18 (c)   Flex. When pressure is applied to the mid-section of the ski, it bends like an archer's bow.

Ski Maintenance

The base and edges deteriorate with wear and tear, and need regular maintenance. This can be done yourself, or left to a specialist workshop. Detailed ski maintenance lies outside the scope of this book, but the main objectives are summarized below:

Bases   Rocks and stones can gouge the bases, causing increased friction and making the skis harder to turn. With use, they can also become 'railed', so that the metal edges stand proud of the base. This makes turning even more difficult.

The plastic base material can be patched or filled to restore its original condition. Gouges under the foot have more effect than those near the extremities. Similarly those beside the edges are more critical than ones that are close to the mid-line.

Railing can be dealt with either by flat-filing to bring the edges level with the base, or by building up the base material to bring it back flush with the edges. Some skis also have a centre-groove running along the mid-line of the sole. This is quite normal, and gives slightly better straight-line stability.

Waxing the bases also influences the skis' performance. This is more important in soft, wet or fresh snow than in hard, icy conditions. The best results are obtained by hot waxing, where the wax is melted onto the bases. Unless the snow is very icy or coarse, it should last for a day or two. Rub-on or spray-on wax can also be used, but this only lasts for a few runs. Many skiers believe that waxing is only important for experts: 'I go fast enough as it is – I certainly don't want to wax my skis to make them go even faster!' is a common response. However, a ski which slides well also turns easily. Especially in soft snow, speed control is easier if your skis are appropriately waxed than if the bases are sticky.

Edges   The metal edges should form a sharp right angle for good grip. (Some skis with 'radial' or 'trapezoidal' edges are ground to an angle slightly sharper than 90°, but the principle remains the same.) In normal use, the edges become blunt. Rocks and stones speed up the process

EQUIPMENT CHECK

Once the edges have been sharpened, they also need to be 'tuned', i.e. dulled off a little at tip and tail. If the extremities are too sharp, the skis become twitchy and hard to control. By dulling them for a short distance (5–15cm back from the front-most point of contact, and about 5cm forward of the tail) the skis grip more uniformly and turn more smoothly.

and create burrs. This impairs both grip and turning. The skis are first flat-filed or machined, to smooth the edges and remove burrs. They are then filed along the side-walls to sharpen them back to a clean right angle.

Ski preparation should be appropriate for the conditions. Very hard or icy snow requires sharp edges for grip, but the state

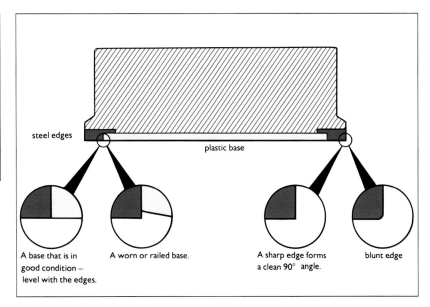

steel edges

plastic base

A base that is in good condition – level with the edges.

A worn or railed base.

A sharp edge forms a clean 90° angle.

blunt edge

Fig 19   The base and edges.

Fig 20   Sunset in Val d'Isère.

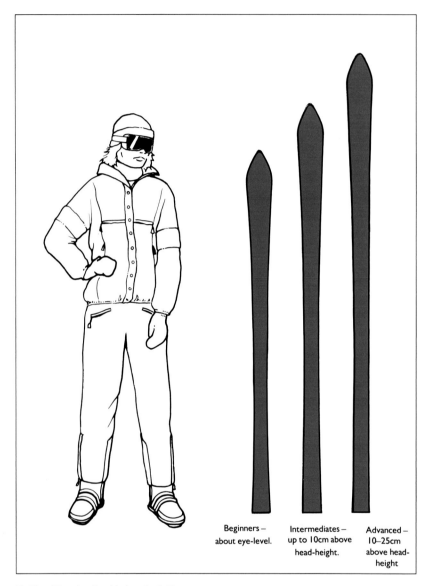

Beginners –
about eye-level.

Intermediates –
up to 10cm above
head-height.

Advanced –
10–25cm
above head-
height

Fig 21   Choosing the right length of ski.

information, magazine reviews and ski-shop staff. Having selected a suitable model, the other main consideration is the appropriate length. The following is a general guide:

- Complete beginners – about eye-level.
- Early intermediates (linked turns on easy runs) – between eye-level and head-height.
- Good intermediates (skidded parallels on moderate runs) – between head-height and 10cm above.
- Advanced skiers – 10–25cm above head-height.

Ski length is related to weight as well as height: a heavy person needs a longer ski; a light person, a shorter one. Most manufacturers publish charts showing the length recommended for your height, weight and standard of skiing.

Carrying Skis

When carrying skis, it's easy to accidentally hit other people with them. In the open, the best way is to carry them on your shoulder with the tips in front and pulled well down. Make sure you don't turn around suddenly when carrying them like this. In confined spaces, they should be held vertically with tips uppermost. Skis are much easier to carry if they are securely held together. The ski brakes usually interlock, but rubber or webbing ties are useful when walking any distance. Alternatively, you can use your poles to form a carrying handle, provided it's not too crowded.

Ski Poles

Ski poles have a variety of purposes: propulsion; getting up after a fall; maintaining balance; and timing and support in more advanced turns. Their main features are:

- A tip which bites into the snow. Modern poles have safety points, which are serrated or cup-shaped tips that give purchase on icy snow, without the risks of a single sharp point.
- A plastic disk – the basket – to stop

of the bases is less critical than in soft snow. By comparison, soft snow requires less edge-sharpness but better base preparation.

Choosing Skis

Each model of ski is designed for a particular performance level, and is meant to be used in a particular length. Some people think that by buying a high-performance ski in a short length, they will get good grip and control without the demands of a full-length ski. In fact it's much better to choose a model designed for your ability. Its performance should match your needs more closely than one which was made for a more advanced skier.

Even then, the choice can be daunting. Apart from trying them out, guidance can be obtained from manufacturers'

Fig 22 (a)   *When carrying skis on your shoulder, keep the tips in front and pulled well down.*

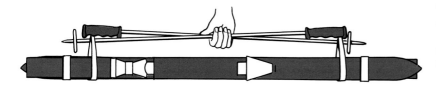

Fig 22 (b)   *Using the poles to form a carrying handle.*

the pole penetrating deeply into the snow. Baskets should be replaced whenever they become badly worn or damaged.

● A handle, which may come in one of two basic designs: sabre or strap. Straps are more common and are convenient for beginners. Sabre grips are preferred by some skiers because of their positive support. They may also be marginally safer in certain situations.

The correct length has your forearm parallel with the ground when planting the pole. Because it sinks in up to its basket, length can be checked indoors by holding

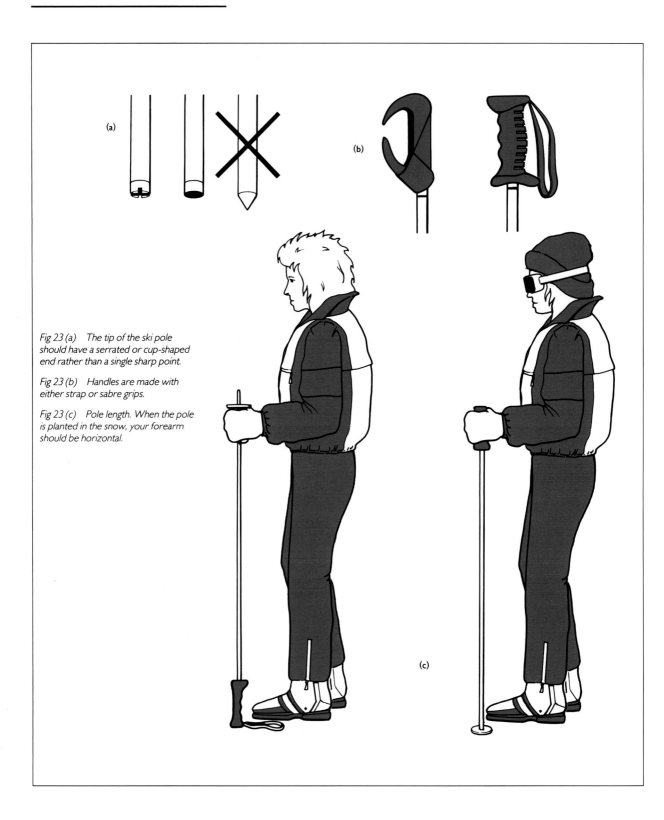

Fig 23 (a)   The tip of the ski pole
should have a serrated or cup-shaped
end rather than a single sharp point.

Fig 23 (b)   Handles are made with
either strap or sabre grips.

Fig 23 (c)   Pole length. When the pole
is planted in the snow, your forearm
should be horizontal.

the pole upside down beneath the basket. Standing upright, your forearm should be horizontal when the handle touches the ground. Beginners benefit from slightly longer poles. At this stage they are used mostly for pushing, getting up after a fall and to aid balance. An extra 5–10cm gives greater leverage and support.

Most poles have grips with broad, flat tops. These should be at least 5cm in diameter, to minimize injury if you fall on your pole. In particular, they should be bigger than the eye socket. Racing grips often have much smaller tops, but are not designed for recreational use. Some poles also have offset or 'corrective angle' shafts or grips. These allow a firm pole-plant with less strain on the wrist, which many skiers find beneficial.

Bindings

Bindings are designed to play a dual role. Firstly, they must hold the boot firmly to the ski, to provide a positive steering linkage. Second, they must release at a predetermined force, not only to reduce the risks of a broken leg, but also to guard against torn muscles, ligaments and tendons. Most bindings are step-in designs, with separate toe- and heel-pieces. Their basic release action is sideways at the toe and upwards at the heel. Some also have additional directions of release – diagonally or vertically upwards at the toe, and diagonally at the heel.

Two other key components of the binding are the anti-friction device and the ski-brake. The anti-friction device or AFD is a small pad immediately behind the toe-piece, designed to minimize friction between boot and binding in a sideways release. Ski brakes consist of spring-loaded arms which dig into the snow when the ski is released, to stop it sliding downhill. When you step into the binding, the arms are retracted clear of the snow.

The information which follows is not intended to turn you into an expert on bindings. Rather, it's to help you understand how your equipment works, so you can recognize problems and have them professionally dealt with.

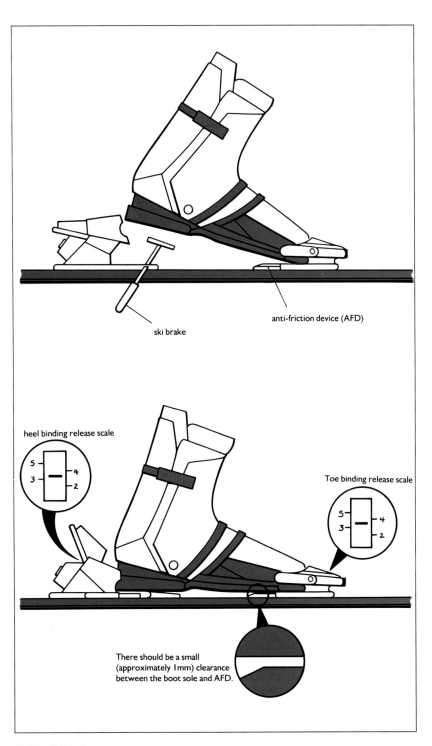

anti-friction device (AFD)

ski brake

heel binding release scale

Toe binding release scale

There should be a small (approximately 1mm) clearance between the boot sole and AFD.

Fig 24   Ski bindings.

Binding Adjustment

Release settings depend on your height, weight and ability. Most bindings use an internationally agreed scale of settings – the DIN scale. Bindings set to the same DIN number should release at the same force, provided the other adjustments are correct.

Two other adjustments are critical if a binding is to operate effectively: forward pressure and toe height. Because of the skis' flexibility, bindings need lengthways elasticity. Otherwise, when the ski bends, the boot would become jammed between the toe- and heel-pieces. This is achieved with an internal spring which presses the heel-piece forward against the boot. For it to function correctly, not only must the boot fit into the binding, but the forward pressure must also be accurately set. Because boot soles may vary in thickness, the height of the toe-piece is adjustable. Most bindings should have a small clearance between boot sole and anti-friction pad, which must be accurately set.

Some bindings also adjust for toe width, heel height and boot-toe position. These have less bearing on the safe operation of

the binding than the DIN setting, forward pressure and toe height. In any case, binding adjustment and maintenance should be entrusted to a trained ski technician.

Binding Safety

Apart from correct adjustment, there are three other factors which influence the bindings' operation:

● While the anti-friction device may become scuffed in normal use, it must be free of gouges, mud or grit.
● Where they contact the bindings and AFD, the boot soles must be smooth, clean and free of major wear.
● Before stepping into the bindings, the boot soles must be free of snow.

Ski Brakes

While bindings are important for your own safety, ski brakes are vital for the safety of others. It's not only inconvenient to have to retrieve a runaway ski; without an effective brake, it can travel fast enough to cause serious injury to others. You can check the brakes yourself. Without a boot

in the binding, the brake arms should spring downwards firmly enough to raise the tail of the ski off the ground. With the boot in place, the arms should retract above the ski's top surface. Any problems should be referred to a ski technician.

Choosing Bindings

For maximum reliability, bindings are best used near the middle of their adjustment range. If your correct setting is DIN number 5, it's better to choose a model which goes from 3 to 8 rather than one which goes from 5 to 10.

The second principle is to buy the best you can afford. It's much better to economize on skis than on bindings. While cheap skis may not perform as well, they don't compromise your safety. Also, a good quality binding can be transferred to new skis when you upgrade them. This is especially important for children. Their bones are softer than those of adults, and a greenstick fracture is harder to set accurately than a clean break. The quality, adjustment and maintenance of bindings is vital in order to protect young bones and joints.

CHAPTER 3

PHYSICAL PREPARATION

This chapter outlines the main aspects of fitness and preparation which need to be considered. For more specific training advice, *see* Further Reading.

While you don't have to be in the peak of physical condition, it pays to prepare yourself before going skiing. Although the activity itself is not especially strenuous, the mountain environment places a number of demands on your body. Also, the risks of injury are significantly lower for someone who is in good shape. Stronger muscles are more resilient; greater flexibility protects joints, muscles and tendons from injury; overall fitness reduces the likelihood of accidents caused by fatigue.

Even with good physical preparation, psychological factors also have a strong bearing on your performance. Self-trust and your approach to learning can significantly affect progress. Anxiety and fear reduce enjoyment, create muscle-tension and increase the likelihood of accident and injury.

Chapter 1 covered a number of issues to improve your mental approach. Some of these can be developed before going skiing; others can be used at the time, to increase your ability to get the best from yourself.

STAR TIP

Probably the question I'm asked most often is how I explain my consistency in ski racing. Some people have said that tests show I have extraordinary athletic gifts. This is not so. But I am convinced that mental attitude has a lot to do with winning.

Ingemar Stenmark
Skiing Magazine, 1981

Heart and Lungs

The mountain environment can sap your energy and cause fatigue before you have even put your skis on. To guard against it, the main aspect of fitness is the condition of your heart and lungs.

Altitude

The majority of recreational skiers spend a large part of their lives close to sea-level. Because most resorts are high up in the mountains, your body must adapt to altitude. The main factor is reduced air pressure. Each breath supplies less oxygen than at sea-level so that even at rest, your heart and lungs must work harder than normal. The higher you go, the greater the effect. At 1,000m – the height of many Alpine villages – the demands are 12 per cent greater than at sea-level. At 2,400m there is a 33 per cent overload, while at the top of Europe's highest lift station, at 3,840m, the figure is 61 per cent.

Therefore, regardless of your ability, it's important to improve the condition of your heart and lungs. That's especially true for beginners, who expend more effort than experienced skiers in walking, climbing and getting up after falls.

Climate

As well as altitude, the climate itself puts an increased burden on the body's resources. Temperatures of −20°C are not uncommon. If it's windy, the rate of cooling is speeded up even more. On a clear day, the air is often much drier than at lower altitudes. When you're out skiing, it's therefore important to drink plenty of (non-alcoholic!) liquids. However, in mist or low cloud, humidity levels can be very high. Moist air saps body heat much faster than when it's dry, increasing the cooling effect still further.

To guard against this, an important consideration is your clothing. But even when you're dressed for the conditions, your body is better able to cope if you are fit and well-nourished. Once again, the main factor is cardio-respiratory fitness – the condition of your heart and lungs. Blood and nutrients must be circulated throughout the body to keep it warm and functioning effectively. Poor conditioning speeds up the onset of fatigue and the effects of cold.

The best way to improve your cardio-respiratory fitness is with prolonged, gentle exercise. Swimming, jogging or cycling are excellent. The aim is to raise your heart rate for several minutes with a moderate, sustainable workload rather than tiring yourself with brief, energetic bursts of activity.

Strength and Endurance

While skiing doesn't require great physical strength, there are certain groups of muscles which must be in good condition for safety and enjoyment.

Because of the flexed posture of skiing, the thigh muscles (quadriceps) work harder to support your weight than when standing upright. They also comprise the springs of your suspension, absorbing undulations in the terrain. Finally, they provide much of the power for the actions of turning – moving from one foot to the other; pressuring and unweighting the skis.

While the legs work actively to cope

upper arm and shoulder muscles

abdominal and back muscles

thigh muscles

Fig 25   Muscular strength and endurance for skiing.

with the terrain and to make the movements of turning, the upper body should remain quiet, with little movement or disturbance. The abdominal and back muscles are the main ones which stabilize and balance the upper body. Because the most common loss of balance is backwards, the abdominal muscles are most frequently involved in recovering control.

The upper arm and shoulder muscles are also important, especially for beginners – when walking, pushing along on the flat and climbing uphill. When getting up from a fall, the gentler the slope the greater the effort that's involved. Here too, beginners need to prepare by strengthening their arms and shoulders.

The main consideration is muscular efficiency. You don't need to develop bulging muscles; rather, tone and endurance are the main factors. To that end, exercises which involve moderate loads over an extended period are therefore better than brief bouts of heavy activity.

Flexibility

Unlike ballet or gymnastics, the actions of recreational skiing don't involve a large range of movement. However, muscles are more efficient when operating well within their range of movement than near the limits. Also, falls and recoveries can create some very extreme positions. Both to guard against injury and to minimize fatigue, flexibility is therefore vital. Because strengthening exercises eventually produce reduced mobility, it's important to use a stretching routine after every session. These should be gentle and progressive. Take the joint to its limit of movement and hold it for several seconds, rather than forcing it with quick, jerky actions.

Agility

As well as being physically prepared for the task, your confidence and fluency of movement can also be enhanced. Agility is the ability to move quickly and react

appropriately to the situation. It's involved in all sorts of activities: tennis, football, gymnastics, cycling and running on rough ground all require the ability to respond in a quick, adaptable way. In any particular sphere, agility is partly a matter of knowing the precise movements or techniques required, but more generally, it's about having the confidence and quickness of movement to react. That can be developed in many sports and activities.

Several sports have features in common with skiing. Skating, skateboarding, waterskiing and surfing all involve balancing on a moving platform. They not only develop general agility, they also provide a foundation for many of the movements of skiing. To steer a ski, you must tilt it onto an edge. The same is true in these other sports – the legs are tilted towards the direction of the turn. While the actions differ in detail, the general principles transfer readily from one activity to another. Therefore, as well as developing overall fitness and agility, participation in other sports can help provide a useful basis for improving your skill.

Artificial Slope Training

Britain has a large number of artificial ski centres which are open all year round. These not only enable beginners to learn the basics of the sport before going to the Alps; experienced skiers too can use them to maintain and develop their skill.

For beginners, one of the most important elements is equipment familiarization. Having got used to wearing ski boots, you will be much better able to choose one that fits well when you're in the resort. Knowing how to put on and take off your skis can save a lot of time and effort during the first few days.

After a few hours of lessons, you should be able to use a ski lift and control your descent down gentle runs. With a moderate investment in time and money,

Fig 26   Opposite: Wayne Watson and Jean Zimmer skiing in unison.

Fig 27 (a)–(d)   A stretching routine.

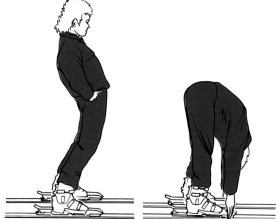

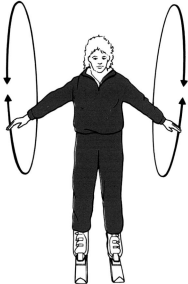

Fig 27 (a)   Hamstring stretch. Using your sticks for support, slide one ski forward and the other one back. Gently press the hips forward and down to stretch the back of the leg. Repeat twice with each leg.

Fig 27 (c)   Stretching the lower back and pelvis. With hands on hips, circle your pelvis round as big an arc as you can. Go round five times in one direction, then five the other way.

Fig 27 (b)   Spinal stretch. Put your thumbs against the small of your back and, keeping your legs as straight as possible, push your shoulders back and your hips forward to arch your lower spine. Then bend forwards, bringing your head as close to your knees as you can. Repeat twice.

Fig 27 (d)   Shoulder circling. Circle your arms fives times forwards then five times backwards, taking care not to push the arms back too hard on the rearmost part of the circle.

Fig 28   Having fun in the powder.

a course of artificial slope lessons can bring you to the level of skiers who have already spent a week on snow.

For experienced skiers, it's important first to get used to the medium. While the techniques are the same, the response of the skis is less positive and precise. For that reason, you should start by going back to basics. Spend the first half-hour just ploughing and plough turning to get the feel of the surface.

It's possible to reach an extremely high standard on artificial slopes. You can not only use them to get back to where you were at the end of your last ski trip – with practice and commitment, advanced parallel skiing, bumps and racing techniques can all be learned as well.

Finally, artificial slope skiing can improve your approach to the sport. Without the distractions and demands of an alien environment, you can gain confidence as well as developing sound technique.

On the Mountain

To function at its best, your body must be warmed up prior to activity. It's the same as the engine of your car – until reaching its working temperature, it's less efficient and more prone to damage. By warming up, the blood flow to the muscles is increased for greater efficiency. By then doing some stretching exercises, flexibility and resistance to injury is improved.

It only takes a couple of minutes before your first run of the day. By jogging on the spot or climbing briskly uphill, your pulse-rate and breathing are increased. After that, go through a few stretching exercises such as those in Fig 27 to loosen up the legs, spine and arms. Do each exercise slowly and gently, without straining or using sudden movements. Always do your warm-up immediately before skiing; if it's done before a long lift ride, its value is lost. Make sure you are in a safe, sheltered spot; apart from the risk of collision, it has little benefit if it's done on a cold, exposed mountainside.

At the end of the day's skiing, a brief warm-down minimizes the chances of becoming stiff and sore. The same stretching exercises can be used, followed by a gentle jog on the spot, shaking out the arms and legs to loosen off the muscles.

PART 2
BASIC TECHNIQUE

CHAPTER 4

FIRST MOVES

First Steps

The first thing to learn after putting your skis on is how to move about. Your feet have grown to about six times their former length. What's more, they no longer grip very well. Instead, they slip and slither in every direction.

EQUIPMENT CHECK

Ski length is very important for effective learning. At this stage, your skis should be below head-height. For beginners, the ideal length is between shoulder and eye-level.

It's important to start on completely level ground. You need a smooth, level area about 10m by 5m, so you can get used to moving around without tripping or sliding away.

The Fall-Line

For most of our lives, we're accustomed to having a firm purchase on the ground. That's what makes the banana skin such a strong comic motif – it removes the very foundation of our stability. Moreover, in a world that provides good grip, we needn't be attuned to slight changes of gradient. But after putting on a pair of skis, a barely perceptible slope suddenly becomes a major issue. It's important to recognize what is happening, and deliberately look more carefully at the surface you are standing on. It's not that you can't see the gradient, you just don't normally look with such care.

When hanging a picture on a wall, you can easily see when it's out of true. You have a keen eye for detecting angles and

Fig 29   The fall-line. The skier's tracks snake symmetrically to either side of the fall-line, which itself is the most direct route downhill.

slopes, even if you don't use it very often. That's the eye you need for skiing, rather than the one you use for walking down the street.

From any point on a slope, there's a particular line that a stream of water follows – the steepest, most direct route. It's not necessarily a straight line – in a curving gully, the water takes a snaking path down the centre. In skiing, that path is called the 'fall-line'. The term 'flow-line' is also sometimes used, although that has a slightly different meaning as you'll see later. It does, however, describe skiing's form of motion beautifully.

Walking

Going in a straight line is easy. It's just like ordinary walking except you don't have to lift your feet. To walk forward, simply

slide one foot then the other. It's best to begin without ski poles. At first, co-ordinating the arm-swing is quite hard. The action is the same as in walking – the opposite arm and leg swing forward together – but it's easier after having got used to the gliding forward step. There's hardly any friction on snow, so you can only push forward very gently as you walk. Once you have learned the arm action, you can push with your poles as well.

Turning Corners

When changing direction, you must take account of your elongated feet. Turning your toe inwards or out simply crosses the skis; instead you must step out to the side as well, putting the skis into an A or a V shape (looking down from above). The V shape is more useful when walking on the

flat, but the A provides control when sliding downhill. Perfecting the movements now will stand you in good stead later. The clock turn is a good exercise:

1. Step the skis around 360°, first keeping the tips at the centre of the clock-face, then the tails. Try to use only ten or twelve steps.
2. Try turning through 360° in only five or six steps.

Use a figure-eight circuit to practise these. Try alternating V and A steps. Speed the movements up, slow them down, and experiment with lengths of stride. A fast, powerful V stride feels similar to skating.

Loosening Up

It's important to gain confidence in the equipment while on the flat, before you start sliding downhill:

Fig 30   When walking, simply slide one ski forward then the other. The poles can be used to help push you along. The opposite arm and leg swing forward together, as in normal walking.

Fig 31 (a) and (b)   The clock turn. On level ground, practise turning through 360° using both A and V steps. Make sure you step out to the side so as not to cross the skis.

(a)

(b)

1. Bend down as if to adjust your boot-clips.
2. Lift alternate skis off the snow.
3. First lift only the tail, then only the tip, then the whole ski.
4. Throw a glove up in the air and catch it while you are walking.
5. Step sideways like a crab, keeping your skis parallel the whole time.

Then try some more dynamic movements while standing on the spot:

1. Jump the skis off the snow, landing as softly as possible.
2. Jump only the tails into the air, then only the tips.
3. Jump the tails out into an A shape, then back to parallel.
4. Jump the tips apart into a V shape and back again.

Fig 32   A figure-eight circuit on level ground. This gives practice in walking and changing direction while wearing skis.

Fig 33 (a) and (b)   Static exercises. To gain confidence and familiarity with the equipment, try a variety of movements while standing on the spot.

(a)

(b)

Fig 34 (a) and (b) To increase confidence and mobility, try some more vigorous movements while standing on the spot, for example, jumping the skis into the air and jumping the tails apart into an A shape.

(a) (b)

Side-Stepping

Walking straight uphill doesn't work with skis on, as they just slide backwards. Instead, stand at right angles to the fall-line and walk up sideways, using the same crab-like side-step you tried earlier on the flat. The skis must stay at 90° to the fall-line, otherwise they will slide forwards or back. That's why you must switch to 'picture-hanging mode' to see any changes of slope direction or contour.

If the skis slip sideways, gently move your hips towards the hill. Reaching your downhill hand as if to pick up a suitcase has the same effect. The skis tilt over so their edges bite into the snow, reducing the tendency to slip. This action is a fundamental principle of skiing. Leaning the leg sideways tilts the ski onto its edge, giving the sensation of lateral grip or resistance. The ski remains free to slide along its length, but the tendency to slip sideways is reduced the more it is edged:

Fig 35 Side-stepping. On a slope, keep the skis exactly 90° to the fall-line. To prevent them slipping sideways, step onto the little toe of the uphill foot, the big toe of the downhill one.

Fig 36 (a) and (b)   Herringbone. Notice the skier's wide gait to prevent the ski tails from getting crossed. As the ski edges bite into the snow, they leave a characteristic 'herringbone' pattern.

(a)   (b)

THE SKI-WAY CODE

When climbing uphill, always keep well out of the way of other skiers. Unless it's very wide, you should always climb up at the sides rather than in the middle of the slope. If you're walking or climbing without skis on, it's especially important to keep to the edge of the slope. Footprints in the snow create a hazard which can cause injury to others.

1.   Take a few paces up the slope. Use the edges for grip, stepping onto the little toe of the uphill foot, the big toe of the downhill one.
2.   Now turn towards the fall-line with small A steps. As you turn, the skis start sliding downhill.

Right now, you're a 'ballistic skier', able simply to aim and go, with no correction or control *en route*. That will soon change,

but for now it's important to choose an area where you can practise safely and confidently without brakes or steering.

Herringbone

There's another method of climbing, called herringbone because of the pattern it

---

KEY POINT

In herringbone, the skis only grip sideways. They will still slide along their length, and can slip backwards across each other in the V. Therefore, when standing on a slope, you must keep gently pushing your feet apart. When climbing, you must push off at right angles to the ski rather than straight uphill. It's the same when ice- or roller-skating. Like skates, skis only grip sideways. Push diagonally forwards in the direction the ski is pointing, not straight ahead.

---

leaves in the snow. It is slightly harder to do, so start by practising on the flat:

1.   Step your skis out into a V shape and walk forward, keeping the V as you go. Take fairly big strides and use a wide gait, otherwise the ski tails get crossed.
2.   Once you're used to it, take a few paces up a gentle gradient. On a slope, the V stops you slipping backwards. If you do slip, push your knees and hips towards the hill, tilting the skis further onto their edges. As with side-stepping that makes them grip.

Turning Round on a Slope

Having climbed up with side-step or herringbone, you must turn round to set off downhill. You need to get lined up in the desired direction without sliding away until you're ready to go. There are two methods: either using your ski poles for support, or by gripping with your skis.

At this stage, the ski poles can be an added encumbrance. Since you've already learned how to grip the slope with herringbone, let's first do it without poles. Facing uphill in a V shape, the skis tend to slide diagonally towards each other. That's easily resisted by gently pushing your legs and feet apart. When facing downhill, the same principle applies, only now the skis must be in an A shape.

If the angle is the wrong way round, the skis slide apart instead of together. You can't exert nearly so much force to pull your feet inwards, and when they go their separate ways, the results are both uncomfortable and undignified. Just make sure that the arrow formed by the V or A points in a downhill direction. That way the skis will always slide towards one another rather than apart:

1.   Having climbed uphill with herringbone, turn to face across the slope. Keeping a wide V angle (between 10 and 15 minutes on the clock-face), turn round on the spot until your downhill ski is across the fall-line. Use small steps to turn around. If you tend to lose the V, take a bigger step with the leading foot, a smaller step with the following one. Once the downhill ski is across the slope, you can bring the uphill one parallel, to stand as if you had side-stepped up the hill.
2.   Step the uphill ski out into a wide A shape and, using the same small steps as before, turn round till you're facing directly down the slope. As long as you maintain the A, the skis can grip. If they slide forward before you're ready, push your heels outwards and gently sit back towards the hill. That makes the edges bite harder, just as in side-step and herringbone.
3.   When you're ready to go, stand up and forward to release your grip on the

Fig 37   Turning round on a slope without poles. As you step round towards the fall-line, keep the skis in a wide A shape to stop them sliding away. The edges bite into the snow in the same way as when climbing uphill using herringbone.

snow. As the skis start sliding, they gradually run parallel. If they tend to cross, move your knees apart slightly as you set off. Once in motion, imagine you're standing in the swaying corridor of a train. You can't control its motion, but provided you're loose and alert, you can remain balanced as it travels along.

THE SKI-WAY CODE

Before setting off, always look round to check that no one is coming. Although the slower skier has the right of way once they are moving, it's your responsibility not to ski out in front of someone else.

Fig 38   As you release your grip, the skis start to slide and gradually run parallel.

Fig 39 (a)–(c)   Turning on a slope.

Fig 39 (a)–(c)   Turning round on a slope using poles for support. When setting off, make sure you resume a normal grip on the poles.

(a)

(b)

(c)

You can also use your poles for turning round:

1.   With your skis across the slope, reach the poles as far downhill as possible.
2.   Put your hands on top of the grips and dig the points in about 60cm apart.
3.   Leaning against the poles, turn round with several A steps.

Provided your poles are directly below your skis, you can hold yourself without sliding away. As you set off, lift the poles and grip them normally as you start to move.

KEY POINT

With hands on top of the grips, elbows locked straight and arms in line with the poles, your skeleton takes most of the load. As soon as anything goes out of alignment, however, your muscles have to take the strain. As you step the skis around, make sure they keep pointing towards the poles. That way, your support is always in line with the direction that the skis want to slide.

Having the poles wide apart aids stability, and leaves a gap for your skis to slide through. Make sure the poles point backwards as soon as you start moving – if they point forwards, you might run into them if they catch in the snow.

First Tumbles

Falling over while learning to ski is as inevitable as getting wet when swimming. To minimize the risk of hurting yourself, there are a few points to bear in mind:

Falling Over

Give in to the inevitable. When you lose balance, don't fight it. If you're tense – either from anxiety or through trying not to fall – you'll have a harder landing and may strain a muscle. Instead, just relax and let yourself go.

Especially in the early stages, most falls are backwards or sideways into the hill. If you feel yourself falling, sit down alongside your skis. If you go straight backwards, roll to one side, otherwise you'll toboggan downhill on the tails of your skis. Whichever way you fall, straighten your legs as you hit the ground. If your legs remain bent, the knee joints are much more vulnerable, especially if they dig into the snow. Straightening your legs also acts as a brake, helping the skis swing round below you into position for getting back up.

If the snow is soft and powdery you can practise falling over. On hard or wet snow it's much less appealing. In that case, imagine the action instead. Mental rehearsal is a powerful learning tool. Picture the action in your mind's eye: sit down gently into the hill and, as your hip touches the snow, kick your feet out sideways. Go through it several times now and at intervals later on. It's surprising how automatically you react after this 'imaginary practice'.

It's also important to protect your hands and arms. If you're not carrying ski poles, cross your hands over your chest, so you land on your hip and shoulder. If you are carrying poles, keep a firm grip on them to stop your fingers getting hurt.

Getting Up

Once on the ground, you must be systematic about getting up again. If the skis are pointing even slightly downhill, they will slide away the moment you start getting to your feet. Switch into picture-hanging mode to get the skis accurately positioned across the slope.

It's much easier if you're lying uphill of your skis. If your body is below your feet, swing round into the right position. From there, crouch forward and tuck your feet

Fig 40 (a) and (b) Falling over. When you feel yourself falling, relax and let it happen. Aim to sit down to one side of your skis. As your hip touches the snow, kick both legs out straight.

(a)

(b)

KEY POINT

When getting up from a fall, the secret is to keep your legs as bent as possible until your body is above your feet. With straight legs, you have to lift yourself much higher before you are balanced.

in close to your hips. The aim is to get your hips over your feet with the minimum movement or effort.

If you aren't carrying poles, push up sideways with your hand. Make sure you push at right angles to the skis, otherwise they'll slide. With poles, there's a more efficient method:

Fig 41 (a) and (b)   Using your poles to get up. First get your skis across the fall-line. Squat as close to them as possible. Dig your poles in next to your uphill hip. With your downhill hand over the top of both handles, push yourself upright with both arms.

(a)   (b)

First put your downhill hand over the handles. Then, with your other hand just above the baskets, put the points in the snow beside your hip and lever yourself up with both arms.

A problem with both methods is that they depend on arm strength. While there is also a knack to it, some people simply lack the power in their arms and shoulders. That's more often true of women than of men.

By contrast, women often have greater strength in their upper thighs, coupled with greater flexibility. So instead, squat between the skis and, holding on to your knees, pull yourself up forwards. It's important to crouch well forward to avoid putting undue strain on the knee ligaments.

Ultimately, everyone must find their own way of getting up. If all else fails, take one ski off. In the early stages, don't refuse a helping hand, as there's no point

THE SKI-WAY CODE

After falling over, always get up and out of the way as quickly as possible. If you need to spend time putting skis back on, clearing snow from your goggles and so on, move to the edge of the piste before doing so.

exhausting yourself struggling to get back on your feet.

Beginners have the hardest time of it. The steeper the slope, the easier it is to get up, since your body is already higher in relation to your feet.

First Slides

Sliding straight downhill is known as schussing. So far, it's been incidental to

learning to climb back up there again. It's now time to start developing balance and control while travelling downhill.

Skiing is a dynamic, athletic activity. Just like tennis, football, skateboarding, netball or cricket, you need good balance and timing, the ability to make rapid changes of direction and speed, and the versatility to respond to changing situations. The main difference is that you have a pair of elongated, slippery feet. Apart from that, the demands of balance, timing, agility and versatility are common to many other activities. The basis of all these qualities is posture.

Posture

Good skiing posture can be likened to a tennis player ready to receive service, or a goalkeeper waiting for a penalty. The aim in each case is readiness for action. Your

Fig 42   In the early stages, a low 'goalkeeper' stance provides the best balance and mobility.

means of propulsion – to run, jump, swerve and maintain balance – is by pushing against the ground. To do that, your legs must be bent. The more powerful the push, and the quicker the movement, the greater the necessary bend. You can stand much more upright in readiness for a small step than for an all-out dive.

Experienced skiers often stand fairly upright. That's because their anticipation and control are good. Most of the time, they don't need to make sudden swerves or recoveries. Beginners, on the other hand, very often do. Indeed, any skier who is on a slope near the limit of their ability needs a lower, more dynamic stance. To begin with, adopt a fairly flexed, 'goalkeeper' posture. As your skill

EQUIPMENT CHECK

While ski boots are much stiffer than normal footwear, they should allow you to flex your ankles forward without too much resistance. On pressing against the tongues of the boots, the resistance should increase progressively, stopping before your ankle reaches its limit of movement. Stiff boots inhibit learning and cause poor posture and mobility. It is important never to slacken the top of the boot to compensate, as this leaves the ankles vulnerable to injury.

improves, you can stand more upright provided the task remains well within your ability.

Agility

The whole point of this stance is to be ready for action – ready to make the movements needed to control your skis. The next task is therefore to get used to moving around while sliding downhill. In an unfamiliar environment, it's normal to act cautiously. When you don't know what to expect, that's a very sensible reaction. In sport, it's usually manifested in a restricted range of movement. Limbs tense up, and movements become jerky and stiff. Think how people move when they first put on ice- or roller-skates. That's exactly what happens in skiing too. The first aim is to get used to moving as freely as before you ever put skis on.

You've already done some loosening-up

exercises on the spot. Now try them while sliding downhill. Make sure that you have an adequate run-out so you needn't worry about stopping. Also, don't climb very far uphill at this stage – it's better to have lots of short runs rather than a few long ones.

The following are some exercises to develop agility and confidence while sliding downhill:

1. Bend down to touch your boots and stand back up again.
2. Pick a glove up off the snow as you slide past.
3. Throw a glove into the air and catch it.
4. Lift one ski off the snow, and then the other.
5. Step sideways to the left and right as you travel downhill.

Once you're confident with the last two exercises, try making a series of small A steps as you're sliding. Just as on the flat,

they let you change direction while moving. Until you've learned to steer properly, use them for avoiding obstacles.

Now try some more dynamic actions while sliding:

1. Jump the skis off the snow, landing as softly as possible.
2. Jump only the tails into the air.
3. Jump the tails out into an A shape, then back to parallel.

Don't worry if you find these last exercises too demanding at this stage; there are other, gentler routes to becoming an accomplished skier. The most important element is to become confident and relaxed while travelling downhill.

Flow and Resist

A universal principle of skiing is summed up in the idea of 'flow and resist'. You've already met the idea of the fall-line – the

Fig 44 More dynamic movements while sliding downhill.

Fig 43 (a) and (b) Agility exercises when sliding downhill: lifting alternate skis off the snow, and stepping sideways.

(a)

(b)

line followed by a stream of water as it flows down a slope. A ballistic skier takes exactly the same route, flowing downhill under the influence of gravity and momentum.

Unlike water, skiers can also resist gravity's pull. You've already learned to resist when climbing and turning round, by pressing the ski edges into the surface to make them grip. Exactly the same applies while sliding downhill, except that here, the grip is not total. It's like the difference between putting the handbrake on to park your car, and braking while in motion. Resistance can vary in degree.

Resistance is what controls a skier's descent. It varies from the all-out skid of a downhill racer after coming through the finish gate, to the gentle turns of an intermediate skier meandering down an easy run.

Fig 45 Ploughing. Push the skis apart into a snowplough while sliding downhill.

Ploughing

If you managed the last exercise of jumping the skis out into an A and back again while moving downhill, you've already experienced resistance. In the A shape, the skis run slower than when they're parallel. It's called a plough, and provides the simplest means of braking and steering.

Learning to Plough

If you're sufficiently confident and athletic, you can develop the technique by jumping out into the A, then holding it as you continue to slide downhill. The skis skid at an angle to your direction of travel, creating resistance which slows you down. If you find the jumping exercise difficult, you can progressively push the skis out when you're sliding. By starting with a good bend at ankles and knees, you can apply a stronger push with less effort. You can try the action right now.

Indoor Exercise
Stand in your stocking feet on a slippery floor. Push your feet out into a shallow A shape, continuing until they're about 75–100cm apart. Hold onto a chair-back, in case you slide too far.

There are two key principles for efficient ploughing. The first is to balance over the balls of your feet as you push out into the A. The further back you're balanced, the more weight is on the tails of the skis, making them harder to push apart. The second is to move your knees apart as you push your feet out. If you go knock-kneed, the ski edges dig in and resist your efforts.

In a wide plough, you may have to stand slightly bow-legged to avoid over-edging the skis. It feels a bit like riding a horse..

Initially, just push out into the plough for the last few metres of each run. Once you have gained confidence, start ploughing from further up the hill. With practice, you can eventually maintain it for the entire descent:

Fig 46 It's impossible to plough effectively with your knees locked together.

1.   Having turned round using the plough, gently release the edge grip by sinking down and kneeling forwards into the boots.
2.   As the skis start to slide, maintain the angle to control your speed of descent.

The resistance created by the edges constantly tries to push the skis parallel. If they're edged too hard, they also tend to cross at the tips. It's important to develop control over the action while ploughing at varying speeds and on different gradients:

1.   Vary the angle as you move downhill. Start in a shallow plough, and sink down to push the skis out wider. As the resistance slows you down, come up into a shallow plough again. Repeat the action rhythmically during the descent.
2.   Start in a shallow plough, but standing in a low crouch. Try keeping your hips at a constant level while pushing your feet out wide then letting them come closer again.

The first exercise uses your body-weight to help push the skis apart, while the second relies mainly on strength. Known as 'weight-method' and 'strength-method', they help increase your control and versatility while ploughing.
   It's not only the width of plough that influences the skis' resistance, but also the

plough angle. Compare the effect over a couple of runs:

1.   Maintain a constant angle as you push the skis apart.
2.   Push out mainly against your heels to create a wider angle.

While the resistance increases in both cases, opening out the angle has a stronger effect.

The Braking Plough

The wider the angle, the greater the resistance. A gliding plough creates minimum resistance; a braking plough creates a lot. In general, the braking plough is used for controlling speed in a straight line, whereas the gliding plough is used for steering. Let's look in more detail at gliding and braking. The exercises which you tried earlier, varying the angle of the plough using weight and strength, also affect the skis' resistance, i.e. they produce braking:

Set off down a gentle gradient with the skis in a shallow plough. This time try braking to a halt. Gradually widen the plough to

increase the resistance, and continue until the skis have stopped.

Try both weight and strength methods for braking. Unless you're on a very shallow slope, you will probably find the weight

Fig 47   Plough braking to a halt. Continue pushing the skis outwards into a wide A shape to create increased resistance. (Compare this with Fig 45.)

method takes less effort. But in order to develop your versatility and feel for the skis, you should practise both.

It's important to recognize the factors that influence how well you can brake. In a car, braking distances are affected by speed, the load carried, and the slipperiness of the road surface. On skis

too, the faster you're going, the harder it is to stop. While your weight doesn't vary, steepness has much the same effect. The steeper the slope, the harder it is to slow up, as if you were carrying a heavy rucksack.

Unlike tarmac, snow is always slippery. However, the skis' grip depends on snow texture and hardness. It's almost impossible to brake on smooth polished ice, even on a very gentle slope. On the other hand, firmly packed powder snow provides excellent grip and resistance.

Gliding

While the plough brake is useful, it's not the main method of stopping. Turning is a much more efficient way to control your speed. For that, you must practise the glide. Unlike a braking plough, the aim is to minimize your resistance:

1. Mark your starting point on the hillside with a ski pole or glove, and see how far you can get in the plough glide.

2. Mark your finish point, and aim to improve your distance.

Make sure the skis don't run parallel; maintain a constant angle while letting them run as freely as possible. It's a good way of developing your sensitivity and edge control.

Finally, try varying the plough angle while maximizing your flow. When you were seeing how far you could glide, you probably ended up using a very shallow plough. Try minimizing your resistance in a wide plough as well.

CHAPTER 5

FIRST TURNS

Plough Turning

When ploughing, you probably found yourself veering off course from time to time. Unless the plough is perfectly symmetrical, the skis naturally deviate one way or the other. In a plough, the skis point in different directions. As a result, they skid diagonally to your direction of travel. Skidding is what produces the extra resistance.

If everything is symmetrical, both skis skid equally. They each resist by the same amount, so you go in a straight line. However, as soon as that symmetry is disturbed, you turn. The ski with more

KEY POINT

It's easy to get mixed up about which leg does what. In the plough, your right ski points left while your left ski points right. In order to turn left, you use the right ski, and vice versa. However, thinking about it in these terms is very confusing. If you are nervous, it's even worse. Think how often people get lefts and rights confused in a driving test. The part of the brain that deals with such things switches off under stress. Programming your actions in those terms makes the task unnecessarily difficult.

Concentrate on feeling rather than thinking. By simply pressing on alternate feet, you discover which one turns you which way. If your actions are governed by feedback, there's far less risk of confusion than if you try to follow a cookery book procedure: 'press on my left foot to turn right . . . or was it left . . . ?' If you tried to drive in terms of 'turn the steering wheel anti-clockwise to go left' you'd have trouble avoiding the traffic. Whereas if you learn by discovery, so the connections are made at the physical level rather than by the intellect, the actions quickly become automatic.

grip dominates. While still skidding, it deflects you in the direction it's pointing. If your stance is lopsided or you're not evenly balanced on both feet, you may deviate from your intended course.

Making Turns

To turn, all you need to do is to alter the amount of grip that each ski has, while maintaining the plough. A simple method is to vary the pressure on each ski. You've already ploughed straight downhill while bending and straightening your legs. This time, bend one leg more than the other, so your weight presses more strongly onto that foot:

1.   As you travel downhill, rhythmically press down on alternate feet, so that first one ski then the other has more weight put on it.
2.   As the pressure shifts from foot to foot, the skis respond by turning slightly. Don't try to turn very far, just make the skis snake gently to either side of the fall-line.

The effectiveness of turning depends on where the pressure is applied to the ski. While turning, feel which parts of your foot and lower leg transmit the increased pressure. Is it the ball of the foot or the heel? Is it along the inside edge of the foot behind the big toe, or the outside edge behind the little one? Is there more pressure against the front of your shin or the back of your calf?

The most effective way of pressuring the ski is through the ball of the foot, against its inside edge. The leg bends from the ankle more than the hip. It's a kneeling rather than a sitting action, flexing the ankle forward so your shin presses into the tongue of the boot.

Indoor Exercise

You can try it now. Put two markers about 60cm apart on the floor, and jump from side to side across them. As you spring sideways, the push-off comes through the ball of the foot. The leg bends mostly at ankle and knee, to absorb the landing ready to push off for the next jump. Plough turning uses the same action, except the movements are slower and gentler. Instead of springing into the air, just move across from foot to foot. You still need a big range of movement, but in slow-motion, like walking on the moon.

Improving Your Turns

Edging

You've already learned to turn by varying the pressure on the skis. However, a ski's grip is determined not only by pressure, but also by how far it's tilted onto its edge. In fact you've already been using the edges too. When ploughing, your feet are further apart than your hips, so the skis are naturally edged. That's an aspect which can be refined:

Set off in a gliding plough and gently move your thighs from side to side. As your knees and hips move across, one ski is edged harder while the other is flattened. The leg action is similar to swinging a golf-club, but without moving the arms or upper body.

The action deflects the skis in the direction you moved your thighs. With a big enough sideways movement, the skis don't actually turn, but instead drift diagonally across the slope. When a ski is edged hard, it bites into the snow and runs along its edge. If you do it while ploughing, you get deflected diagonally, along the line of the edged ski. It's called snowplough traverse.

(b)

(a)

Fig 48 (a)–(c)   Plough turning. As the skier presses down on his right ski, its grip increases. This makes it turn into the direction it's already pointing – towards the skier's left.

(c)

EQUIPMENT CHECK

For effective control, the movements of edging must be accurately transmitted to the skis. Your boots must therefore give good lateral support, while still allowing your ankles to flex forwards. It is also important to fasten the top clips securely. For edge control and to guard against injury, the ankle and lower leg must be firmly held.

The action helps develop edge control, especially in improving your ability to edge the ski strongly. It also illustrates two errors in plough turning – under- and over-edging the skis. A ski that's not edged enough won't grip even with pressure on it. Instead of turning, it just slides sideways. If edged too hard, it won't turn either. Rather than skidding around in an arc, it doesn't skid at all. Instead it continues in the direction it's pointing, in a snowplough traverse.

Skidding is an essential part of turning. While you *can* turn with minimal skid, it's a very advanced technique, known as carving. For now, you should develop your feel for the optimum amount of skid: too much, and the ski just slides away no matter how much you press on it; too little, and it won't turn at all.

Edging is controlled mainly by this side-to-side movement of the thighs. Moving the knee and hip inwards tilts the ski further onto its edge; moving them

outwards flattens it on the snow. These actions enable you to adapt your technique to the conditions. Skis grip less on hard snow; it's like driving on ice compared with dry tarmac. Similarly, skiing faster or on steeper terrain requires more grip.

Even in a single turn, the amount of grip must vary. In the first half of the turn, you're approaching the fall-line and going with gravity; in the second half you're turning away from it and need more grip to resist the pull. Experiment with it:

Fig 49 (a) and (b)   Developing edge control with snowplough traverse. By moving both thighs to one side then the other, the skis drift diagonally across the slope.

(a)

(b)

of actively turning your legs and feet to alter the tightness of turn. It's not a new movement – you've used it since first learning to plough. Ploughing doesn't simply involve pushing the skis apart. The legs and feet must also be turned to create the plough angle. That's the action in question.

As you press down on the ski, you can make it turn more quickly by pushing the tail out into a wider plough. It's like plough braking, but with only one leg at a time:

Imagine squashing an ant under your foot. As you press down, twist the foot slowly in the direction of the turn, as if grinding it into the ground.

A common error is to turn the hips instead of the leg and foot. When pushing the skis into a plough or going from a glide to a brake, your hips can't turn – they would have to go both ways at once. However, when the action involves only one leg at a time, it's easy to turn your hips as well. It's a fault which appears at every level of skiing, in parallel as much as snowplough.

Three problems arise if the hips turn more than the feet. Firstly, the top of the leg moves outwards, flattening the ski and causing excess skid. Secondly, rotating the hips swings the upper body over the inside ski. That shifts your weight off the outer ski, making it skid even more. Finally, the action puts strain on the knee ligaments, making them much more prone to injury. You can see the difference by trying the action in front of a mirror:

Indoor Exercise
1.   Stand as if you're ploughing and rotate one leg and foot. Look at your hips – have they turned too?
2.   Turn both feet inwards at once, so your hips can't rotate. Now turn just one leg at a time, without any hip rotation. The turning foot goes more pigeon-toed, while the hips keep facing the same way.

To sum up, there are three elements involved in steering a ski – pressuring, edging and turning (PET for short). The aim is to apply these elements appropriately to the situation. A manual-shift car has

As you press onto the turning ski, move your thigh inwards to increase the grip. Feel how much is needed – too little, and the ski slides sideways as it turns; too much, and it stops turning as the edge bites too hard.

The action is like a runner preparing to swerve. When sinking down ready to push

sideways, the leg leans into the direction of the swerve. However, while the runner must extend their leg to push off, the skier remains flexed throughout the turn.

Foot Steering
Both pressure and edging are needed to control the skis. One final element is that

Fig 50 (a)–(c)   Tightening the turns with foot steering.

Fig 50 (a)–(c)   As the skier presses down on the ski, he pushes the tail out into a wider plough to create a tighter turn.

(a)

(b)

(c)

three foot-pedals, each with a different function. Driving involves using each of the pedals in the correct degree and sequence for the situation. However, unlike a car, the three ski controls don't work in isolation. You can't use them one at a time. Even the most elementary snowplough turn involves pressuring an already-edged ski which is turned at an angle to your direction of travel.

Therefore, while you can vary the balance between them, they are not completely separate actions. When turning your leg, the ski tends to become edged more strongly. When edging the ski, the pressure on it tends to increase. As you ski, monitor the effects of your actions, so you can tailor them more effectively to the terrain and conditions.

Practice, Consolidation and Refinement

At this point, the main priority is for effective and varied practice. Rather than immediately moving on to the next stage in technique, you must consolidate what you've learned. There are three main objectives:

1.   Learn to adapt the mix of pressure, edging and foot turning to the situation. Long smooth turns on gentle, grippy snow need a different balance than quick, tight turns on steeper or icier terrain. For the former, a gentle increase in pressure is often enough, while the latter requires more edging and foot turning too.
2.   Practice enables your actions to become more automatic. Ultimately they are applied by feel rather than conscious, deliberate intention. The process is helped by 'getting out of your head and into your body'. That is, giving more attention to feeling what your body is doing and less to thinking about your actions.

It can be applied to several different aspects: monitoring your posture and movements; feeling the resultant pressure changes through your legs and feet; and becoming aware of the skis' response in relation to the snow and terrain.

3.   The final objective is learning to read the terrain. Compared to other environments, snow gives little visual information. It's not immediately obvious whether it's soft or hard, wet or dry. Nor are changes in gradient always apparent. Especially on overcast days, snow tends to conceal its contours. Bumps suddenly leap out of nowhere; hidden drop-offs and ridges catch you unawares. While it's sometimes impossible to read the terrain accurately, you can still pick up a great many clues about what is there.

Look carefully at the surface. Is it matt or shiny? Smooth or rough? Are there areas of differing colour? Are other skiers' tracks cut deeply or not? All these variations indicate different snow conditions. When you can't see clearly, use your other senses. Listen to the sound of the skis, to hear the snow-texture. Feel it through your legs and feet – the smooth hardness of ice, the rough crunchiness of frozen snow, the silky glide of powder.

You're learning not only to control your skis, but also to direct your attention. You can focus inwards to your own body to develop sensitivity and technique, or out into the environment to read the snow and terrain. It's best done in that order – first developing and refining your technique, then applying it to different conditions. Stick to easier and more uniform runs at first, and move on to ones with more challenge and variety later.

THE SKI-WAY CODE

At this stage it's especially important to consider the safety of others. Remember that slower skiers have the right of way and that when overtaking you should always give them a wide berth.

Turns and Turning

Having learned to steer, there are two ways of applying it: you can go in straight lines with occasional turns, making a series of zigs and zags down the hillside; or you can link your turns into a continuous flowing curve.

Rhythmic, flowing movements are intrinsically more enjoyable than disjointed ones; that's the main appeal of music and dance. Skiing is just such a dance, with the ever-changing contours of the mountain as your partner. Not only is it more fun to ski rhythmically, it's also easier. It would be difficult to dance without rhythm. When actions are linked, each is triggered by the one before. The link is both model and stimulus, giving form to the movements and punctuation to their timing.

The first turn is always the hardest. Once your rhythm is established, everything is much easier. But if your turns are not linked, each one is a 'first turn'.

STAR TIP

The next time you're riding a chair-lift, look below and pick out the best skiers on the hill – those who make skiing look effortless, who seem to flow with the mountain, linking their turns smoothly and efficiently. Now see if you can determine what these good skiers have in common. Is it the way they hold their arms or make their pole-plants or bend their knees? No, if you look closely, you'll find that the common denominator is that they all make smooth, round turns.

Billy Kidd
Skiing Magazine, 1981

It's not just rhythm that's involved; the forces generated during one turn help initiate the next. They are stronger with higher speeds and more advanced techniques, but the principle applies from the outset. When turning, the outer ski has more pressure on it than when going straight. That's not only because you are pressing on it. It is also due to inertia – the same effect that pushes you sideways when cornering in a car. That pressure bends the ski like an archer's bow. If you run on to a straight line after turning, the pressure decreases and the ski returns to its former shape. However, if you start each turn from its predecessor, you can harness some of the ski's 'spring energy', making your actions easier and more efficient.

The energy stored in the ski rebounds you into the following turn. It's like a running jump compared with one made when standing still. The run-up gives a more powerful spring with less effort. The principle is summed up in terms of 'turns' versus 'turning'. When making turns, you perform separate, discrete actions; when turning, your actions are continuous and linked. That's not to say the rhythm is unchanging – like any skilful dance, it follows both partner and music – but throughout, your movements should link and flow, anticipating the changes in tempo, and altering their cadence to match.

Turning and Body Rotation

Control is strongly influenced by the interaction between legs and body. While the skis follow a snaking track, the upper body should keep facing more directly downhill. The reasons have already been mentioned: if the hips turn too much, edging and pressure are reduced. However, especially if you're anxious, it's very common to rotate your body:

1.   Pick a reference point directly downhill of you, and ski towards it making shallow, rhythmic turns. Imagine it's a penalty spot, and that you are a goalkeeper waiting for the shot. Keep your hands wide and around hip-level, to protect the goal-mouth from a low ball. As you ski towards it, does your upper body keep facing the penalty spot? Once you have identified any body rotation, use the goalkeeper image to help minimize it.
2.   A related exercise for the hips instead of the arms and shoulders is to imagine you have got a spotlight shining out of your belly button. Use the same reference point as before. Does your spotlight keep shining towards it, or does it sweep from side to side as you turn?

It's harder to feel what your hips are doing compared with your shoulders, so it may take longer to identify any rotation that's occurring. Imagine your favourite singer is performing on stage. Your task

Fig 51 (a) and (b)   The 'goalkeeper plough'. Although the legs and skis are turning back and forth across the slope, the upper body keeps facing towards the imaginary penalty spot.

(a)

(b)

is to keep the spotlight on them the whole time.

Bear in mind that these exercises are intended to correct faults, not to define the 'right' way to ski. Unless you're only turning a small way from the fall-line, your hips and shoulders inevitably come round as well. Rather than always facing directly downhill, they should simply turn less than your skis.

Up and Down

Your first turns were made by sinking down onto the ski to increase its grip. Pressuring the skis like this creates a series of up and down movements in time with your turns (see Fig 48). You rise up at the end of one turn ready to sink down into the new one. The 'rebound' mentioned above provides some of the impetus, pushing you up into a neutral position over the skis before you sink down again. Rather than being a series of separate movements, these actions too should flow. If your skis follow a continuous S-shaped curve, the up-and-downs should have a similar sinusoidal shape, superimposed in the third dimension.

Flow and Resist

Pressuring a ski not only makes it turn, it also increases its resistance. In Chapter 4 the idea of flow and resist was introduced. There, it was related to plough gliding and braking. When turning, you're resisting selectively, with only one ski at a time. The increased resistance is what causes the turn. At the end of each turn there's a drop in resistance, before it builds up again from the other ski. In other words, there's a constant cycle of flow and resist: increasing resistance during the latter part of each turn, increasing flow into the start of the next.

The resist phase of each turn is what enables you to control your speed. The further the skis turn from the fall-line, the greater the resistance and the more you slow up:

Feel the changing resistance as you ski, the

sensation of acceleration and deceleration in the turns. Vary its degree: make turns which slow you to a gentle walking pace, others which flow more quickly down the slope.

The more effectively you can modulate your resistance, the better you can deal with changing gradients and terrain. However, on steep slopes even experts have difficulty controlling their speed with plough turns. On runs steeper than the average blue, more advanced techniques are needed.

Up, Down and Forward

Another effect of changing resistance is to disturb your balance. With the drop in resistance at the end of each turn, the skis can accelerate out from under you, making you overbalance backwards. It's more noticeable on steep or icy terrain, where anxiety and muscle-tension increase the effect. Even if you don't fall, the skis become harder to control. They understeer, just like a car when its front wheels fail to grip the road firmly.

Just as in the car, the problem is due to reduced pressure under the front of the ski. There are situations where it can be used to advantage, but here it's just a hindrance. The solution is to bring your body forwards over the skis at the start of each turn. Rebound up and forward from the previous turn rather than straight upwards. It's not a big, obvious movement, and is much easier to feel than it is to see:

1.   Feel the pressure against your feet. As resistance increases towards the end of the turn, the pressure builds up along the whole length of your foot.
2.   As you rise up into the new turn, move the pressure forwards over the balls of your feet.

This up-forwards movement is called projection. As well as giving a smoother, more effortless start to the turns, it's also very exhilarating, as you 'go with gravity' towards the fall-line. The rhythm of turning is matched by the succession of flow and

resist. Provided you project forward to accommodate the skis' initial acceleration, you will be able to stay balanced and ready to resist.

KEY POINT

The action of coming forwards into the turn seems very straightforward, but can be quite hard to learn. That's due to confidence and relaxation rather than technique. Lack of confidence makes you tense up, pushing you back on your heels. Any attempt to come forward is therefore blocked. You must remove the block before you can make the movement:

Practise on gentle, confidence-inspiring terrain. Having mastered it there, you can gradually increase the difficulty of the slope. Check your body. Are you clenching your toes? Are the backs of your calves tight? Your thighs and buttocks? What about the upper body – the small of the back, the shoulders, neck and arms?

Once you have identified any tension, use the relaxation methods described in Chapter 1 to ease it away.

Sideways

So far the emphasis has been on linking your turns. That's generally the most efficient and enjoyable way to ski. But traversing, i.e. skiing across the slope in a straight line, is also an important technique. Traversing is useful in its own right for getting across slopes without losing much height – to reach a restaurant or lift station, or to get onto another run, for example. It's also a good exercise for more advanced manoeuvres.

Snowplough uses only the inside ski edges, whereas parallel skiing uses the inner and outer edges in unison – while one ski is on its inside (big toe) edge, the other is on the outside (little toe) one. Traversing with skis parallel uses the edges the same way:

1.   Maintain your direction at the end of a

plough turn, so you travel across the slope in a straight line. Once your downhill ski is pointing in the desired direction, edge it firmly to hold its line across the slope.

2.   When traversing in the plough, relax the uphill leg to let that ski drift parallel to its partner.

The aim isn't to bring the skis close together; rather, they should be parallel but apart. The closer the skis are to one another, the harder it is for you to balance. Also, with your legs close together, you can't control the edging of each ski independently.

Pressure Control, Weight and Strength

So far you've applied pressure to the outer ski by kneeling against the tongue of the boot, leaning more of your body-weight onto one ski than the other. When travelling faster and over more undulating terrain, you can use other methods of pressure control. In preparation, it's useful to try out one of them at this stage.

Chapter 4 introduced both weight and strength methods of plough braking. They can both be used when turning too. What you've already learned can be thought of as 'weight method plough turning'.

Plough Pumping

With strength method braking, you started in a lower, more crouching stance and pushed the skis out into a wider angle. This time, try pushing out with only one leg at a time. Provided the ski is pushed *into* the snow rather than just sliding across the surface, two things happen as the leg extends: the pressure – this time caused by muscular effort – increases against the ski; and as the ski is pushed further away from your body, the amount of edging is increased. As a result the ski turns. For now it's probably harder work than what you were doing before.

Next, reduce the amount of leg extension. You need not start in quite so deep a crouch, so there is less effort. Instead of extending the leg right through the turn, push out more briefly. It's now a pumping action, as if you were using a foot-pump to inflate a tyre. Push down on the pump and immediately let your foot get pushed back up again.

Set off in a gliding plough. Briefly pump against one ski and relax the leg again. Even though the action only lasted for a moment, the result is a sustained plough turn.

Try a linked series of turns. Find out how

Fig 52 (a)–(c) Running out into a traverse at the end of a snowplough turn.

(a)

(b)

(c)

Fig 53 (a)–(c)   Plough pumping.

Fig 53 (a)–(c)   The skier's right leg is extended with a brief 'pumping' action, momentarily creating increased pressure against the ski. By then relaxing the leg and allowing it to flex, the turn is sustained by the skier's own inertia. Compare this sequence with Fig 48.

(a)

(b)

(c)

small a movement is sufficient to trigger the turns. Provided your basic posture is sound and the leg relaxes immediately after the pumping action, only a tiny movement is needed.

It can be thought of as 'minimalist skiing', using the least amount of movement and effort to make the skis turn. That's achieved by harnessing the forces created as you ski. Instead of only using the power of your own muscles, you're channelling those forces to assist you.

The technical reason why it works is that the pumping action creates a momentary increase in pressure against the ski, enough to make it start turning. As soon as the turn starts, a g-force is produced, due to your inertia. If you now simply relax the same leg while keeping the ski edged, the g-force continues to press your body mass more heavily against that foot, sustaining the turn after the pumping action is completed.

CHAPTER 6

From Plough to Parallel

Pressure Control

So far, only the outer ski has been used for turning. The inside one has simply stayed in the plough in a supporting role. In effect you're a one-legged skier. The next step is to learn to steer the inside ski actively too. But before doing so, it helps if the action of the outer ski is refined.

> **EQUIPMENT CHECK**
>
> At this stage, slightly longer skis may be helpful. Because you're travelling faster and on steeper terrain, the extra length gives greater stability and grip, improving your control. Provided they are designed for intermediate skiers, a good rule of thumb is to use skis which are between head-height and 10cm above.

Whether in snowplough, basic swing or parallel, the outer ski remains dominant. For control and efficiency it needs the greater amount of pressure against it, otherwise it loses grip and drifts away sideways.

Pressuring the Outer Ski

To begin with, focus on what's happening right now:

● What proportion of pressure is on the outer ski compared to the inner one : more than 90 per cent? around 75 per cent? 50 per cent or less?
● Does the pressure increase gradually or suddenly?
● Does it continue increasing until the start of the new turn, or does it level out?

If the pressure on the outer ski is near 50 per cent, try increasing it. However, don't assume that more is always better. While you will lack control with under 50 per cent, the optimum depends on the conditions.

Generally, the harder the snow or the faster you're travelling, the more pressure you need. However, in very soft snow, the skis may veer in different directions or get crossed if there's too much disparity. If the onset is slow and gradual, try applying the pressure more quickly. If there's a delay before the new ski is pressured, shift more directly from foot to foot. Varying these aspects alters the shape and rhythm of the turns.

When the turns link smoothly without a pause, the sensations can be likened to pedalling a bicycle: as soon as you have finished pressing down on one pedal, you start to press on the other:

Focus on this pedalling action. Increase the tempo of pedalling to link your turns closer and closer together. As you do so, the plough itself gets progressively narrower. The extra speed, coupled with the rhythm and rebound from turn to turn, cause a gradual development from plough towards parallel.

Lightening the Inside Ski

So far, the emphasis has been on pressuring the outer ski. The other side of the coin is the reduction of pressure on the inside one. Once again, start by tuning in: Does pressure come off the inside ski at the very start of the turn or part way through? Does it drop suddenly or gradually? Does it stay low right to the end? Once you're aware of what the inside ski is doing, focus on skimming it lightly over the snow:

Skim it through the entire turn. Imagine it's gliding over eggshells, and aim to avoid cracking them.

It's a gentle, relaxed action. The ski doesn't lift – it stays in contact the whole time. Rather than depending on muscular effort, the softer and more relaxed the leg, the better. When you relax the leg, it feels as though it's hanging from the hip-joint. Only its own weight keeps it pressing against the snow. Aim to keep it hanging loose right through the turn. This exercise is especially useful for skiers who use a lot of effort when turning, because it encourages more relaxed and efficient actions.

Pedalling works here too. On a bicycle without toe-clips, the leg that is moving upwards is largely passive. Focus on the passive leg in each imaginary pedal rotation:

Release the pressure against alternate feet by 'switching off' the muscles of each leg as you go from turn to turn.

Starting this exercise in a plough, the plough angle gradually lessens and ultimately disappears. The extent to which it does indicates how effectively the leg has relaxed.

The reason is that ploughing requires muscular effort to hold the A shape. By relaxing one leg, the force which sustained the plough is removed. In going from plough to parallel, aim for gradual change. Progressively increase the degree by which the inside leg relaxes. Take the pressure off that foot earlier and earlier in the turn.

Fig 54 (a)–(c)   By travelling faster downhill and pedalling rhythmically from foot to foot, the plough angle becomes shallower. The result is a half-way stage towards true parallel skiing.

(a)

(b)

Going with Gravity

In Chapter 5, the idea of bringing your body forward at the start of the turn was introduced. There, it was done with an active up-and-forward movement to initiate the turn. The action of relaxing the inside leg achieves the same result.

When turning, inertia pulls you to the outside of the curve. It produces the same centrifugal effect or g-force as in a car, and becomes stronger the faster you go or the tighter you turn. If you swing a weight round on a piece of string and then let go, it flies off at a tangent. Relaxing the old outer leg to initiate the new turn has exactly the same effect. The outer ski grips the snow and deflects you round the turn to create the g-force. Relaxing the leg is like releasing the string.

Your momentum is released along a tangent to its path – diagonally forwards and downhill. That's exactly the direction it must go to keep you balanced over the skis as they accelerate into the new turn. It's quite a scary feeling at first. It takes confidence and commitment for it to work, but when you let it happen, the action of relaxing the downhill leg – the outer one of the preceding turn – has four positive effects:

Fig 55 (a)–(b)   Inertia and the centrifugal effect.

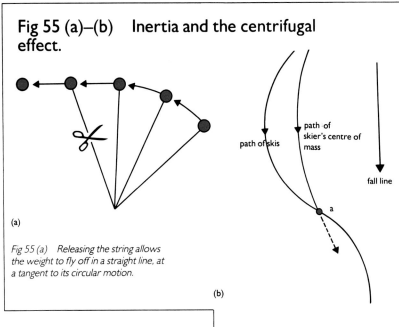

(a)

Fig 55 (a)   Releasing the string allows the weight to fly off in a straight line, at a tangent to its circular motion.

(b)

1. It 'switches off' the resistance at the end of the previous turn, enabling you to flow downhill into the new one.
2. It automatically transfers pressure to the new outer foot.
3. As the leg relaxes, the body crosses the path of the skis, bringing them onto their new edges.

Fig 55 (b)   By relaxing the outer leg at point A, the skier's body is released along a tangent to its former path – diagonally forwards and downhill. It's the same effect as making an up-forward movement to start the new turn.

(c)

(a)

4. It keeps you balanced as the skis accelerate downhill.

The result is smoother and more effortless turning. If you have the confidence to relax and let it happen, the skis feel as if they're starting the new turn by themselves.

Narrower and Steeper

The next step is to put both pedalling exercises together – pressuring the outer ski and skimming the inside one. It's always more effective to concentrate on only one thing at a time. Instead of trying to control each leg separately – trying to do two things at once – the pedalling image merges them into a single, co-ordinated whole.

As you press down on one pedal, the pressure on the other is simultaneously released. The image provides a single task which links the separate movements of your two legs:

Vary the tempo of pedalling. Imagine the bicycle has longer pedal cranks, increasing the range of movement. Check the shape of the action – is it smooth or jerky, 'round' or 'oval'?

Fig 56 (a)–(c)   By dynamically pedalling both legs in unison, the turns follow a tight, positive track. The action also causes the skis to progressively shift from plough to parallel.

(b)

(c)

Bigger, smoother movements make the turns more positive. They're also more efficient – a big movement requires a less intense effort to achieve its effect than a small one.

On steeper or narrower trails, your turns must be more positive and dynamic than on wide, gentle runs. The skis must turn further from the fall-line to control your speed; hesitation or lack of commitment causes loss of balance and control. The increased effectiveness of working both legs in unison – pedalling powerfully from turn to turn – deflects the skis further from the fall-line to give greater speed control. The positive rhythm steers them in a tighter track.

On narrower runs, you also must turn more quickly. Once more, pedalling is an excellent model. Imagine you are cycling downhill. As you pedal, the bicycle gradually picks up speed and the tempo gets faster and faster. Start on easy terrain and see how far you can take it. Increase the rate of pedalling until a wheel falls off. Find out where your limits are, and gradually stretch them. Progressively increasing the rate of turning leads you down a converging, funnel-shaped path. The faster the tempo, the narrower that pathway is.

You can work on it in two ways: you can develop the tempo of your actions by increasing the rate of pedalling; or you can set terrain boundaries, by marking out or visualizing a funnel-shaped pathway on the slope, and skiing within its margins. Both approaches have the same ultimate goal, but an external task like skiing to the converging margins of a funnel has two advantages. Firstly, it distracts attention from your own actions, allowing them to become more automatic. Secondly, it develops the ability to link technique to terrain. By focusing on the width of pathway, your judgement develops along with your technique.

Try it on progressively steeper slopes, too. The steeper the slope, the further you have to turn the skis from the fall-line, to prevent them picking up too much speed.

There's inevitably a trade-off between tempo and extent of turning. The faster the tempo, the less the skis deflect from

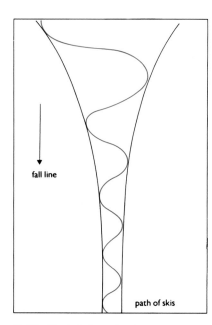

Fig 57   Gradually increasing the tempo of turning takes you down a converging, funnel-shaped path. Visualizing or marking such a path on the hillside and skiing to its margins improves your ability to ski a tight, precise line.

the fall-line. Therefore, the width of funnel you can ski depends on the terrain. The steeper it becomes, the further back you retreat into a wider, more open section of the funnel. You can use these ideas to develop your perception as well as your technique. Look at a slope's steepness: how wide a track do you need on that gradient? How far down the funnel can you go and still be in control? Setting imaginary margins on the hillside is an excellent way to develop your ability to ski narrow trails and improve your eye for a skiable line.

Up and Down

So far in this chapter, there's been no mention of up-and-down movements when turning. That's partly because they are not a necessary element. To pursue the analogy, you can pedal while sitting on the saddle of your bicycle, or by standing on the pedals and moving your body up

and down. On a bicycle, vertical body movements provide more power. In skiing they give tighter, more positive turns. The faster you want to turn, the more you must pressurize the outer ski.

The strongest way of applying pressure is by extending your outer leg. If you push down against the ski to start the turn, your body is lifted up. Then, from the fall-line, you sink back down onto the ski through the second half of the turn. The lower you sink, the bigger the push you can make against the new outer ski to start the next turn. Sinking low also enables you to apply a stronger foot-turning action.

These up-and-down movements should flow with the rhythm of the turns. With the skis following a sinuous S-shaped pathway down the hillside, the rise and fall of your body should form an interlinked series of Ss in the vertical plane.

Edge Control

In using pressure control when turning, the inside leg plays a fairly passive role; the less it does (the more relaxed and lighter it is), the more that ski comes parallel to its partner. But the inside ski can be steered actively too. The first element to consider is edge control. What follows can be used as an alternative route from plough to parallel, or as a way of refining the turns.

Snowplough Traverse

In Chapter 5, this exercise was used for developing edge control over the outer ski. Here it has a similar purpose, but this time for the inside one. In snowplough traverse, one ski is edged harder, deflecting the skier diagonally. Compared with a neutral stance, the other ski is edged less, so the edged one has greater effect.

Feel for this flattening of one ski as the other is edged. Don't overdo it, because if the ski is flattened too much, its outside edge will catch and trip you. This action is the basis of edge-controlling the inside ski of the turn. It's done by pivoting the thigh outwards, and feels as if you're going bow-legged on that side. Just make sure your weight doesn't move across as you

Fig 58 (a)–(d)   Linking the turns.

(a)

(b)

Fig 58 (a)–(d)   By using a big range of vertical movement – finishing the turn by sinking onto the lower ski, then extending strongly against the new outer (uphill) one – the turns link positively and smoothly.

do it, otherwise you end up with too much pressure on the flattened ski:

Monitor the pressure, aiming to keep fairly evenly balanced on both skis. If anything,

(c)

Fig 59   In a snowplough traverse, one ski is edged more strongly while the other sits flatter on the snow.

(d)

the pressure should increase against the more strongly edged ski, as it bites and deflects you across the slope.

Flattening the Inside Ski

After practising with snowplough traverse, try the action when turning. When turning left, pivot your left thigh in that direction; pivot your right one when turning right. If you can't remember which thigh should be doing what, try this:

Imagine your thighs are direction indicators that tell other skiers which way you're going. Like a car, the indicators on the side to which you're turning do the signalling. Turning left, pivot your left indicator out, and so on.

The Edge Change – Basic Swing

Flattening the inside ski enables it to be steered parallel to the outside one. As you move your thigh outwards, pivot your foot. It's similar to the foot-turning action in Chapter 5. There, it was the outer leg and ski which were steered; now it's the inside one. The other difference is that previously the foot was turned to create a wider plough; here it brings the skis parallel.

In order to turn the inside ski, it's no longer enough just to flatten it. Now, the thigh must move far enough to bring the ski onto its outer – its little toe – edge. As the ski changes edge, the leg rotates to bring it parallel to its partner. It's the same 'ant squashing' action described in Chapter 5, except here the foot has very little pressure on it. Try it in front of a mirror:

Indoor Exercise

Stand in a flexed snowplough shape and turn one foot parallel with the other. The leg pivots on an axis between the hip and the ball of the foot.

Watch your thigh as you do it. It moves outwards as the foot pivots. There aren't two separate movements – moving the thigh and turning the foot. Provided your legs are bent, it's all one action.

It's often thought that skiing parallel means skiing with your feet together. However, especially at this level, they should be parallel but apart. They're slightly closer when parallel than in the plough, but should still be around hip-width apart.

Having the skis too close causes two main problems. Firstly, a narrow stance makes balancing harder, with less margin for error. Secondly, you can't control each ski independently with your feet close together, as your legs get in each other's way. With feet about hip-width apart, you can ski parallel without compromising on either balance or control.

Keeping your skis apart is crucial when first learning to bring the inside ski parallel. Bringing the skis together encourages you to pull the inside leg towards its neighbour. However, that tilts the ski more strongly

Fig 60 (a) and (b)   As the thigh moves outwards to change the edge, the leg is pivoted to steer the ski parallel to its partner. Notice that while the skis end up parallel, they remain about hip-width apart.

(a)

(b)

Fig 61 (a)–(d)   Rather than lifting the inside ski to bring it parallel, move the thigh outwards to roll the ski from inside (big toe) to outside (little toe) edge.

(a)

(b)

(c)

(d)

onto its inside edge, sabotaging your aim. Instead, the inside leg must move *away* from its partner, rolling the ski onto its outer edge so it can turn parallel. Rather than bringing the tails of the skis together, pivot under the ball of the foot so that the tips move apart.

At this stage, the inside ski should only be steered parallel in the second half of the turn. To start with, the outer ski is pushed out into a plough and pressured to turn it towards the fall-line, just as before. Then the inside ski is steered to bring it parallel, so that both skis finish the turn in unison. This new turn is called 'basic swing'. It's a half-way stage to parallel skiing. With snowplough, only the outer ski is steered. In basic swing, the outer ski turns alone for the first half, then the inside ski is steered parallel in the second. In true parallels, both skis are steered in unison from the outset.

A common fault is to rotate your hips when turning. Rotating your hips ahead of the skis straightens the inside leg, blocking your efforts to move the thigh across into the direction of the turn. To correct it, slide the inside ski forward as the skis reach the fall-line (*see* Fig 61). The action prevents the hips from turning, which allows the inside ski to come parallel more easily.

From Plough to Parallel – Timing and Foot Turning

Practise the action in linked turns. Once you've established a rhythm, the movements flow together more easily. Focus on their timing by saying 'One' as the outer ski turns, 'Two' as the inside one comes parallel. Is the timing of the 'One' and 'Two' equal on both sides? If not, even them up.

If one leg doesn't work so well, practise snowplough traversing on that side. For the moment, each turn should divide into two roughly equal halves : the 'One' signalling its initiation; the 'Two' as the skis cross the fall-line. From here the action can be gradually developed into true parallel skiing. The only difference between basic swing and parallel is that in basic swing, the 'One' and the 'Two' occur consecutively; in parallels they are simultaneous.

It takes practice to become sufficiently confident and relaxed that your actions link smoothly from turn to turn. For now, don't try to master anything new. Just concentrate on enjoying your skiing: ski long, continuous runs on easy terrain; take in the scenery as you ski; hum a tune and ski to the rhythm.

Once the actions have become fairly automatic, focus once more on their timing. On an easy slope, tune in to the 'ones' and 'twos'. While turning at a fairly constant rhythm, gradually reduce the time-lag between steering the outer and the inner ski. Start with 'one . . . two' then 'one . . two', 'one . two', 'one.two', until eventually they're simultaneous. Alter the timing in small, easy steps rather than in one great leap. As the time-lag between turning the two skis is progressively reduced to zero, the new technique emerges.

Another way of moving from plough to parallel again uses the principle of gradual change:

1. Start off with big, rounded basic swing turns, linking each turn smoothly with the next.
2. Gradually increase the tempo, to make progressively tighter (but still rounded) turns.

As the tempo increases, the delay between steering the two skis gets shorter and shorter. It not only leads towards parallel skiing, but also develops the ability to turn more tightly and quickly. Once more the skis follow a funnel-shaped pathway down the hillside. It's a useful exercise at all levels of skiing. If you can snake down a narrow corridor on gentle terrain, try it on progressively steeper slopes.

One final exercise in this context is to use a shallower and shallower plough angle for turning. This time, focus on the extent rather than the timing of your actions:

Gradually reduce the amount by which the outer ski is steered. During the plough phase, make the skis form a progressively shallower angle.

Your skis don't come any closer together during the parallel phase – it's only in the plough that they are not so far apart. Gradually the plough angle diminishes until it vanishes completely.

Edge Control, Skidding and Stopping

Speed control comes from a combination of three factors:

1. The width of plough. There's less resistance with skis parallel than in a shallow gliding plough, which in turn gives less than a wide plough brake.
2. Your line. This applies both to traversing and turning; the shallower the traverse, or the further the turn continues from the fall-line, the slower you go.
3. The amount of skid. This is actually what governs resistance when ploughing too, but I want to consider parallel skidding separately. Within limits, the greater the amount of skid, the greater the skis' resistance.

Each of these factors contributes to speed control. Of the three, ploughing is the least efficient. The wider the plough, the more effort is needed to maintain it. It's also inappropriate if the aim is parallel skiing. The other two factors normally work together. The further the skis turn from the fall-line, the more they tend to skid. The effect can be used for stopping as well as in linked turns. By turning the skis across your direction of travel you can skid to a controlled halt.

Side-Slipping

A useful exercise for developing edge control is a technique known as side-slipping. It's a good way of negotiating steep, narrow or difficult sections of terrain, and of moving slowly downhill.

You can either side-slip directly down the fall-line, or diagonally from a traverse.

Direct Side-Slipping
1. Stand with your skis at right angles to the fall-line.
2. With your poles behind you on the uphill side, push yourself slowly downhill while keeping the skis across the fall-line.
3. Once you can control your descent, try it without pushing. If the slope is fairly smooth and steep, you can initiate the slip by simply sinking onto your downhill foot. If the skis are reluctant to slip, shuffle them gently back and forth to help them move.
4. Practise side-slipping at varying speeds. By shifting your weight back and forth along the skis, you can also control the direction of the slip, swinging gently back and forth across the fall-line as you descend.

Diagonal Side-Slipping
When traversing, the ski edges bite firmly into the snow to carry you straight across the hill. By releasing the edge grip from a traverse, you side-slip diagonally:

Standing fairly tall on your skis, set off on a shallow traverse. Now sink onto your downhill foot, so that the skis begin to slip sideways while still moving across the slope.

When you want to stop the side-slip, stand tall again. In both direct and diagonal side-slipping, the downward movement causes a slight flattening of the skis to release their grip. By standing up again, the skis are edged harder to halt the slip.
    Practise varying your rate of side-slipping; experiment with different angles of traverse. One common fault is that if your uphill ski flattens too much, its lower edge will catch in the snow and stop it slipping. Aim to keep most of your weight on the downhill ski, so that the uphill one can slip freely while remaining moderately edged.

Skidding to Stop

What follows can be applied in two ways: as a specific technique for stopping and as a more advanced exercise in edge control. Both are equally useful.

Fig 62   Direct side-slip. To begin with, push with your poles to make the skis slip.

Fig 63   Diagonal side-slip. The skier's track shows the direction of motion downhill.

Fig 64 (a)–(c)   Skidding to stop from a plough.

Fig 64 (a)–(c)   Notice that the legs and feet pivot much further than the upper body.

(a)

(b)

(c)

The easiest way to begin is with the movements of basic swing. The key action is that of turning the inside leg and ski:

Set off downhill in a gliding plough. Once you have gained speed, sink down onto one ski while turning the other one parallel. But instead of steering the skis round an arc, let them skid sideways until you come to a stop. The skis may initially follow a curved path, in what's called a swing to the hill rather than a diagonal skid. By shifting your point of balance back slightly – from the ball of the foot towards the heel – you can correct the tendency.

As you start skidding, pick a target in your direction of travel and continue skidding towards it. Practise your accuracy, skidding diagonally downhill in a straight line.

When side-slipping, the skis were only edged by a small amount, whereas now they are edged much more strongly. That's because in the skid to stop, you start with more momentum. The skis must therefore be edged harder to resist it.

If you've a preference for one side over the other, practise the weaker one to redress the balance. Once you're skidding confidently in each direction, try varying its duration:

1. Prolong the skid as far as possible.
2. Stop as quickly as you can. Don't

Fig 65   Opposite: Suzanne Goodwin showing good posture and anticipation as she initiates a turn.

(c)

(b)

(d)

initiate the skid too violently, or you may trip. Increase the resistance gradually and smoothly to a peak rather than applying it all at once.

3. Set a target and practise stopping precisely beside it.

Now try it with skis parallel throughout. Set off on a steep traverse rather than straight downhill, so the skis are already on their edges ready to skid:

1. Just as when side-slipping, start in a fairly tall posture with skis parallel and about hip-width apart.

2. As you begin turning the skis across your direction of travel, sink down into a low, stable crouch.

Once you're skidding, your body should continue facing downhill of the skis. The body shape is as if you're in a tug of war. In a tug of war you're resisting a force. The same is true when skidding – you're resisting your own momentum. Rather than being specific to skiing, the body shape is part of your everyday repertoire of movement. To get the feel of the action, try it with a partner:

Fig 66 (a)–(d)   Skidding to stop from parallel.

Fig 66 (a)–(d)   As in Fig 64, the upper body keeps facing the direction of travel. Notice the 'tug of war' body shape during the skid.

(a)

Reverse your grip on the poles, and have them pull you downhill. With your partner in a reverse snowplough, control the rate of descent by varying the resistance of your skid.

A key point is the position of your feet. They must be apart for stability, but they should also be separated in a fore-and-aft direction. You can illustrate it indoors right now:

Indoor Exercise
1. Start in a 'goalkeeper' stance facing straight ahead.
2. Pivot your legs and feet to point to one side. When they have turned at right angles, they are separated fore and aft by the same amount by which they were apart to start with.

Provided you pivot each foot independently, they become separated automatically. To counteract any tendency to rotate your hips and shoulders, slide the top ski forwards as you turn your feet – the same action as was used to correct the habit in basic swing. You can do it both in a skid to stop and when being pulled downhill by a partner. It not only increases your stability, but also keeps your body facing downhill of the skis in that tug of war posture.

Fig 67   Resisting the pull of another skier. Compare the body shape with the final photos of Fig 64 and 66.

PART 3
ADVANCED TECHNIQUE

CHAPTER 7

PERFECTING PARALLELS

Eliminating the Stem

One route from plough to parallel is by gradually altering the timing with which the skis are turned. Initially, the outer ski is steered at the start of the turn and the inside one brought parallel in the second half. By turning the inside ski earlier and earlier, the actions eventually switch from being consecutive to simultaneous. But 'consecutive' is a much looser idea than 'simultaneous'. The first only requires the actions to occur in the right order; for the second they must happen at the same instant. Skiing parallel needs much more accurate timing than basic swing.

Many experienced skiers have a small stem – steering the outer ski slightly before the inside one, to create a momentary plough as the turn begins. It can be a difficult habit to eliminate, but it doesn't just happen by accident. It's intimately linked with other aspects of your skiing.

Fall-Line Phobia

If you're nervous of a slope and want to turn as quickly as possible, stemming is a positive help. But having developed the habit on difficult slopes, it often persists even on easy terrain. Before dealing with any underlying emotional causes, let's start by working on the quick-turning habit itself. Choose an easy slope, and do some medium-sized turns:

Stretch out the first half of each turn. Take longer to turn into the fall-line, then run straight downhill for a moment before continuing into the second half.

You need to finish the turns more positively to cope with the extra speed from the first half. But the initiation can be much gentler. Instead of using lots of foot-

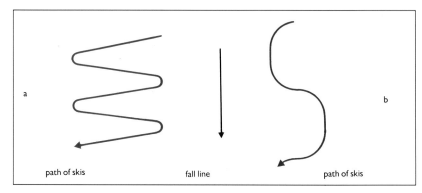

Fig 68   To overcome the quick-turning habit, practise stretching out your turns. Instead of zigging and zagging down the slope (A), let the skis run down the fall-line for a moment before finishing each turn (B).

turning, just emphasize the up-forward movement as you pressure the outer ski.

Stemming is closely linked with excess foot-turning. If the skis keep crossing the fall-line quickly, you're turning them too hard. Feel for what you're doing – once you've identified it, it's easier to modify your actions.

However, if your efforts to stretch out the turns simply cause anxiety, you must also deal with the fear factor. To begin with, is the slope too steep? If not, are there other features that worry you – ice, other skiers, bumps, a blind drop-off? Anxiety is more easily conquered on slopes that don't worry you. Having practised these more rounded, stretched-out turns on gentle runs, try them on progressively more difficult terrain.

Another approach is to gain confidence when schussing. Choose a wide, quiet slope with a good run-out, and decide how much of it you can confidently schuss. Even if it's down near the bottom, start from that point. Then gradually work your way further up the hill. The aim isn't to push yourself to the point of abject terror;

rather, it's to increase the range of speeds and slopes on which you feel confident.

Flow and Resist

Another factor which contributes to stemming is the acceleration in the first half of each turn – the tendency towards greater flow. In Chapter 5, the principle of coming forwards to start each turn was introduced. Without it, your balance shifts back onto your heels.

Stemming is one way of dealing with the problem. In itself the stem creates resistance, reducing acceleration. Also, stemming makes it easier to control the turn if you *are* back on your heels. Forward projection of your upper body reduces the need to stem. It maintains your balance as the skis accelerate, and helps them turn into the fall-line more smoothly and easily.

However the stem originated, it's important to recognize that you can't simply get rid of it – you must put something else in its place. It's not just a bad habit but a functional, integrated element of your technique for which you must find a replacement.

Triggering the Inside Ski

In most situations, the outer ski dominates the turn. In plough, basic swing or parallel, it provides most of the control and grip. However, to help eliminate the stem, focus on the inside leg and ski. Initially just tune in to it. Feel the reduction in pressure as the turn starts, the transition from inner to outer edge as the leg rotates.

Pay particular attention to the timing of the actions: Does the pressure come off right at the start of the turn? When does the edge get changed – at the start, or part-way through? If there's a delay, aim to eliminate it by initiating each turn with the inside leg and ski. While the outer one still provides most of the control, trigger its action by unweighting or edge-changing the inside ski.

You have already used these elements in going from plough to parallel. Deal with them one at a time, focusing on the fine detail of your timing:

1. Take the pressure off the downhill ski at the very start of the turn, before doing anything else.
2. Start changing the edge of the downhill ski an instant before the uphill one.

The Pole-Plant

So far, no mention has been made of the pole-plant when initiating turns. While it's sometimes introduced at an earlier stage, it can distract attention from the development of effective leg action to control the skis.

Co-ordination and Timing

One of the pole-plant's purposes is timing. Because parallel skiing requires much more precise timing than plough or basic swing, the pole-plant can be used as a trigger or 'punctuation mark' to initiate the turns.

First you must sort out which pole to use. It's a classic point of confusion, with

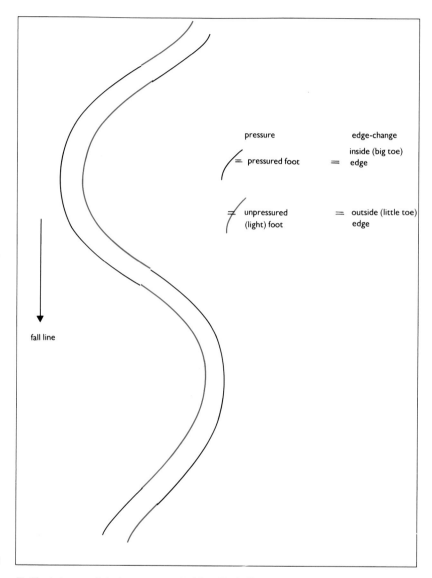

pressure

/ = pressured foot

/ = unpressured (light) foot

edge-change
inside (big toe)
= edge

= outside (little toe)
edge

fall line

Fig 69   In true parallels, the pressure and edging of both skis starts to change at the very beginning of each turn.

lefts getting mixed with rights, the inside being mistaken for the outside hand. First let's put it in a way that your brain can understand, even though your body may not: the pole is planted with the downhill hand, i.e. the one that's going to be on the inside of the turn. So when turning right, you plant your right pole, when turning left, your left one.

One method of translating that into

action was introduced earlier – direction indicators that show which way you're about to turn. This time the ski pole is the direction indicator. Instead of flashing it, you plant it in the snow.

New actions often interfere with other aspects of performance. For a while, the rest of your technique may deteriorate. To begin with, don't link your turns. Keep them widely spaced, and make a direction signal as you start each one. Say to yourself 'Turning left . . . NOW! . . . turning right . . . NOW! . . . ', and plant the appropriate pole on each 'NOW!' Don't worry about precisely how or where the pole gets planted. Just focus on the basic co-ordination and timing: is it early, late, or right at the start? If it's out of time, work on planting the pole simultaneously with the start of each turn.

Refining the Action

The next step is to refine the movement itself. You're not harpooning fish, just pressing the pole firmly into the snow. If you raise your hand too high, it brings your shoulders back and arches your spine. That disrupts balance and control as you finish the previous turn.

The hand and arm position of the 'goalkeeper' stance can also be described as 'holding a hoop'. The hoop is carried below hip-level, and is held at about ten minutes to two – a small distance in front of its diameter. From there, the hand lifts slightly up and out, bringing the pole perpendicular to the snow. The hand only rises enough to bring the point clear of the surface.

Many skiers release their grip with the lower two or three fingers, so the pole pendulums forward into the plant. If it's simply being used a timing aid, that doesn't matter. But the pole-plant has other purposes too: as a balance support, and as a temporary anchor to stabilize the upper body. These require a more positive grip. Keep hold with all four fingers, but without squeezing it to death. Imagine that you're picking up litter. The pole-plant should be firm enough to pierce an empty cigarette packet, but without squashing it flat.

Immediately after the pole-plant, the hand may get left behind. If that's not corrected, it rotates your body into the direction of the turn. As you plant the pole, punch your hand forward and down. That returns the hand to its earlier 'hoop-holding' position, so your body keeps facing towards the outside of the turn. It's like changing down from fourth gear into third. The gear-lever is pushed forward, pivoting at its lower end. The speed of the action depends on your velocity – it's a snappy, punching movement when going fast.

Fig 70 (c)   Immediately after the pole-plant, the hand is returned to its former position on the hoop.

(c)

Fig 70 (a)–(c)   The pole-plant.

Fig 70 (b)   From the hoop, the hand is lifted up and out to plant the pole.

Fig 70 (a)–(c)   To begin with, just think of it as a direction indicator that tells other skiers which way you're turning.
(a) 'Holding a hoop'.

Fig 71 (a)–(c)   As the pole is planted, the hand punches forward and down to return it to its position on the hoop.

(b)

(a)

While the pole-plant itself is a brief, simple action, several problems can arise:

1. Reaching the hand too far forward. This action turns your shoulders uphill, pushing your downhill hip out. It flattens the downhill ski, making it skid and over-steer just before the start of the new turn.

Instead, reach straight downhill. That increases your edge grip at the end of the turn, ready for a positive initiation of the new one.

2. Lifting your hand too high. This brings your shoulders back, disturbing your balance as the skis accelerate into the new turn. Instead, lift it just enough to bring the pole perpendicular without catching. From there, you only need a small downward movement to plant it.

3. Leaving your hand behind after the pole-plant, thus rotating your body. This causes excess skid, and a tendency to fall into the hill. Use the gear-change action to counteract it. As the hand punches forward, keep reaching it down the fall-line through to the end of the turn.

The Purpose of the Pole-Plant

At first the pole-plant may seem more trouble than it's worth, feeling like a completely arbitrary and unhelpful action. But once established, it brings a variety of advantages:

1. Improved timing (as mentioned earlier). Just as a conductor's baton co-ordinates the orchestra, the pole-plant acts as a punctuation mark to co-ordinate your turns. It provides a brief, precise moment of contact, as a focus for the timing of all the other elements.

2. Improved balance. In basic swing, the skis are pushed into a wider stance at the start of each turn, so just as you begin changing direction you acquire a wider, more stable platform. When skiing parallel, there's no such assistance. Instead, the pole-plant provides an outrigger. It gives a momentary balance support, just as the skis roll from one set of edges to the other at the start of the turn.

3. A more positive projection. It supports your body as you 'fall' into the new turn,

before the skis swing round beneath you. This is especially important for quick turns on steep terrain, and in bumps.

4. It briefly anchors your upper body to Planet Earth. Where powerful foot turning is required, the pole-plant provides a point of leverage. It stops your body rotating, allowing you to pivot your legs in the desired direction.

Movement and Motion

Your interpretation of a situation strongly influences your actions. That's as true in skiing as in other walks of life, but especially where the understanding of technique is concerned. For example, if skiing's ultimate goal is seen as keeping your feet clamped together all the time, you'll ski very differently than if you're seeking maximum precision and control.

As well as the details of where your feet, hands or hips should be, there is a more general level at which skiing can be interpreted in one of several different ways. In the early days of the sport, it was often thought of in terms of body positions: the schussing position; the snowplough position; the traverse position; and so on. The actions of skiing were seen as transitions from one position to another. As skiers increasingly came to link their turns, the idea of movements rather than positions became more common. Up-movements, rotations, counter-rotations and down-movements all entered the vocabulary of the sport, as the actions became smoother and more fluid.

However, it wasn't until skiing became understood in terms of its underlying mechanical principles that the most accurate picture began to emerge. That viewpoint is perhaps best summed up in the phrase 'movement in motion'. When travelling downhill, skiers experience a variety of forces. Some are the direct result of their own movements – pressing down on a ski, tilting it onto its edge, and so on – but others also arise from their motion downhill, from the fact that they have momentum. Putting pressure on a ski

that's in motion gives a very different result than when at rest; the effect of edging a ski is very different at 5 and at 50km per hour.

In other words, the effects of your body movements can only be fully understood in relation to your motion downhill. A fixed movement can produce widely varying results; the same result can be achieved with widely differing body movements. The results of your actions depend on external factors. As well as snow texture and terrain, they depend on your speed and direction of motion.

Therefore, skiing certainly isn't a matter of adopting particular positions, nor is it simply a case of performing certain movements. Rather, it involves making movements while in motion. Only by taking both into account can skiing be fully understood.

Anticipation

The first action to be considered in this light is what's called 'anticipation'. Here, the word is being used in a narrow technical sense, rather than the broader meaning of 'anticipating what's about to happen', which involves perception and judgement. It refers to keeping your upper body facing more directly downhill than your skis. At the end of a turn, the skis may have come a long way past the fall-line while the upper body continues to face more steeply downhill. The term comes from the fact that the upper body anticipates the following turn; it faces into the direction in which the skis are about to be steered.

In general, your body should face downhill of your skis as the turn finishes. What's less clear is by how much. One explanation is in terms of how quickly the skis are turning – the sharper the turn, the greater the anticipation. Another, more accurate perspective, is in terms of the skier's motion. A skier's centre of mass (corresponding roughly with the position of their navel) follows a pathway somewhat inside that of their skis. It's the same for a cyclist. To maintain balance, they must lean inwards to counteract their inertia while turning. As a result, the skier's (or the cyclist's) centre of mass follows a

Fig 72 (a) and (b)   Anticipation.

Fig 72 (a)   At the start of a short-radius turn, the body faces more or less directly downhill.

Fig 72 (b)   When making a long-radius turn, the body keeps facing more in the direction of the skis.

more direct pathway than their skis (or wheels).

Watch an expert making tight, short-radius turns. Looking from below, their body appears to be travelling straight downhill while the skis snake rhythmically from side to side. Far from being an illusion, that's exactly what happens – the centre of mass moves straight downhill, while the legs pivot and pendulum to either side. On medium-radius turns the same is also true, but now the centre of mass is also deflected from side to side. It still follows a more direct path than the skis, but no longer a straight line. In long, slow turns a skier has relatively little inertia. Much less inward lean is, therefore, required to maintain balance, so the path of the centre of mass is only slightly inside that of the skis.

In everyday life, we usually face the way we are going. Skiing is no exception. But the skier's body faces the direction in which *it's* travelling, which may differ from the trajectory of the skis. In Chapter 6 the tug of war image was introduced in connection with skidding to a halt (*see* Fig 66). To resist efficiently, the upper body faces in the direction of the opposing force or, when skidding to stop, in the direction

Fig 73   When turning, the centre of mass leans inwards, following a path inside that of the skis.

of your momentum. When turning, the same principle applies. Your momentum tries to continue in a straight line, while the resistance created by your skis deflects it round a curve.

To resist efficiently, your upper body faces in the direction of its momentum. In other words, it faces the direction your centre of mass is travelling, independently of the path of the skis. The orientation of your upper body is therefore intimately linked to the path of your momentum. In some situations it should keep facing straight downhill; in others it should be almost square to the skis the whole way round the turn. So there's no such thing as the 'correct position'. Which way your body should face is not a rule you can learn; rather, it's arrived at by feel.

To ski well requires sensitivity to many things: the feedback from your legs and feet; information about the terrain ahead; your internal sense of balance. It also involves awareness of the path of your centre of mass, feeling the trajectory of your body as it repeatedly crosses over the path of your skis.

The Flow-Line

This crossover occurs just as one turn ends and the next begins. It's the basis of projection – the forwards and downhill movement of the upper body as the new turn begins. It was first introduced as an up-forwards movement to help initiate the turns. But, from the current perspective, it's not so much a separate movement, more a matter of letting your body follow its natural line of momentum. In Chapter 6, it was described under the heading 'Going with Gravity'. In fact it's not simply gravity that you are going with, it's also your own momentum.

At low speeds and when turning gently, the effect of your momentum is small compared with that of gravity. At high speeds and in tight turns, the situation reverses, and momentum becomes the dominant factor. Therefore, at low speeds, it's gravity you must resist; at high speeds it's your momentum. The direction of your momentum is known as your flow-line, in contrast to the fall-line down which gravity

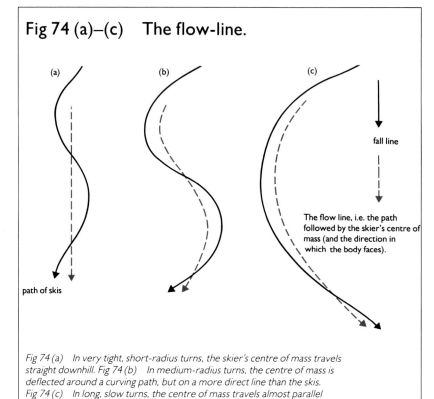

Fig 74 (a)–(c)   The flow-line.

(a)   (b)   (c)

fall line

path of skis

The flow line, i.e. the path followed by the skier's centre of mass (and the direction in which the body faces).

Fig 74 (a)   In very tight, short-radius turns, the skier's centre of mass travels straight downhill. Fig 74 (b)   In medium-radius turns, the centre of mass is deflected around a curving path, but on a more direct line than the skis. Fig 74 (c)   In long, slow turns, the centre of mass travels almost parallel to the skis, but still on a slightly more direct path.

acts. While the fall-line is constant on a given slope, the flow-line is determined by your motion – by the path of your momentum.

You need to develop awareness of your flow line. As you initiate each turn, feel your body cross the path of the skis,

following its line of momentum and 'going with the flow'. At higher speeds and on steeper slopes it's a really exhilarating sensation. The feeling is almost like weightlessness, like going into free-fall at the start of the turn, before your skis begin deflecting you into the new direction.

Angulation and Inclination

One final issue concerns the forces acting on a skier. These vary due to the skier's motion downhill, and must be accommodated by body movements in order to remain in balance.

First there's the effect of inertia. If a turn's arc is constant, so too is the centrifugal effect. Then there's gravity. Even in a perfectly symmetrical turn, the effect of gravity varies from start to finish: as the skis approach the fall-line,

Fig 75   Colleen Bourke enjoying herself on spring snow.

they approach the direction of gravity's pull, but in the second half of the turn they are deflected progressively further away from the direction in which gravity wants them to go.

The forces acting on the skier, therefore, increase progressively during each turn. While the inertial component may remain constant, the effect of gravity builds up throughout the turn. In the first half of the turn, the skier really does 'go with gravity'; it helps rather than opposes the change of direction. In the second half the skier must resist its pull, to continue turning into the hill.

The further you turn past the fall-line, the more strongly you must resist. So the amount of edge grip must progressively increase. Edging comes from leg-lean – from

inclining the legs towards the centre of the turn. There are two ways to produce leg-lean: by banking the whole body over; or by bending from the waist so that as the legs lean in, the upper body leans out. The first is called inclination; the second, angulation.

Angulation is the tug of war action described earlier. It causes a progressive increase in the amount of edging as the skis are steered through the turn. Because of the centrifugal effect, all turns also need a degree of inclination. That's why your centre of mass takes a more direct line than the skis. However, because of the build-up of forces, the amount of edge grip must increase through the turn.

By continuing to incline your body further inwards for increased edge grip,

you'll eventually fall over. The pressure eventually shifts onto the inside ski of the turn, so the outer one breaks away. Angulation, on the other hand, lets you sustain pressure on the outer ski while increasing the amount of leg-lean.

Indoor Exercise

1. Stand in a flexed 'goalkeeper' position, and turn both feet about 45° to the left.
2. Without increasing the pressure on your left foot, try 'edging' both feet. To do so your hips must move back. To stay balanced, your shoulders must simultaneously drop forwards, so the action is one of folding at the waist.

Projecting your body downhill automatically creates inclination. Your centre of mass

(c)

(b)

(d)

Fig 76 (a)–(c)   The skier projects his body downhill into the direction of the turn. That creates inclination, as in Fig 76 (c).

Fig 76 (d)–(f)   The hips then drop down and inwards for increased angulation. Just as when skidding to stop (see Chapter 6), this allows him to resist the build-up of forces towards the end of the turn.

(e)

(f)

Fig 76 (a)–(f)   Inclination and angulation.

(a)

crosses the path of the skis, tilting them onto the new edges. As the turn continues, the hips must progressively drop inwards to produce angulation, increasing your edge grip to resist gravity in the second half of the turn. Turning, therefore, involves both inclination and angulation. While the amount of inclination may stay fairly constant throughout the turn, angulation increases progressively from start to finish.

Finally, there's the relationship between gravity and momentum. As noted above, momentum may have a small or large effect compared with gravity, depending on the speed and tightness of turn. In fast, tight turns, the centrifugal effect becomes much more significant than gravity. Therefore, you need more edge-grip right from the start. Inclination can only provide a limited amount of leg-lean before you overbalance. In tight turns you may therefore need angulation right from the start, for effective grip and control.

CHAPTER 8

SKIDDING, CARVING AND CHECKING

Skidding and Carving

Most turns involve a considerable amount of skid. That is, the tails of the skis follow a wider path than the tips. It's the same as when the back of a car skids on a bend, sliding outside the line taken by the front wheels. Carving, on the other hand, involves turning with minimal skid. To do it, the ski must be bent into the same arc as the turn, while the edge grips firmly the whole way round. The entire length of the ski then follows exactly the same track, leaving a single groove cut into the snow.

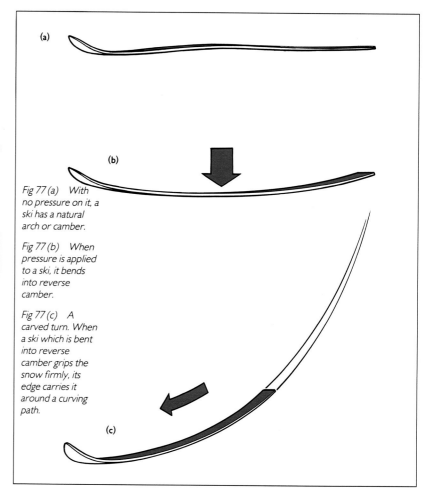

Fig 77 (a)   With no pressure on it, a ski has a natural arch or camber.

Fig 77 (b)   When pressure is applied to a ski, it bends into reverse camber.

Fig 77 (c)   A carved turn. When a ski which is bent into reverse camber grips the snow firmly, its edge carries it around a curving path.

EQUIPMENT CHECK

With no pressure on it, a ski has a natural arch or camber which raises the mid-section up off the snow. When it's bent the other way, the ski is in what's called reverse camber.

Whenever pressure is put on a ski, its camber is flattened or reversed. That's true in both skidded and carved turns. However, to carve, the ski must form a precise arc, so its flex pattern is more critical. You therefore need skis which are designed for the job, i.e. advanced- or 'sport'-level skis (although not necessarily a competition model).

The edges must also grip effectively. Hardpack requires sharper edges than soft snow; when it's very icy, even the sharpest ski may not grip well enough to carve. Finally, the ski must be long enough for good stability and grip. At this stage, you need skis 10–25cm above head-height.

In fact, most 'carved' turns involve some skidding. It's a matter of degree rather than all-or-none. Indeed, skidding is a vital element of control, as it's the most effective means of braking. A ski that's carving perfectly creates no more friction than one that's going straight. While there are other factors which cause deceleration when turning, these are insignificant compared with the effect of a skid.

Think how quickly skiers can skid to stop. Downhill racers have about 100m to stop in after the finish gate, from speeds of over 100km per hour. But while skidding provides speed control, carving has benefits too. Just as in a car, it's harder to steer a precise line when you're skidding; the greater the degree of skid, the less precision you have. Carving, on the other hand, enables you to achieve great accuracy. A ski that's riding an edge can be aimed within a few centimetres. All that's lacking is the brakes.

While a fast, precise line may be fine on open slopes, speed control is much more important in steep, narrow gullies. To ski skilfully requires the ability both to carve and to skid, or rather, to vary the balance according to the situation.

Carving and the Racing Snowplough

The fundamental elements of ski control are pressuring, edging and foot-turning. Every turn consists of a combination of these elements, with the balance between them determining the type of turn. Skidding is generally initiated by foot turning, whereas carving is created by applying pressure to an edge. On a scale from pure skid to pure carve, skidding to stop represents one end of the spectrum. The task here is to explore the other end of the scale.

It may seem odd to use such a basic manoeuvre for advanced technique, but the most effective way of learning to carve is in a plough. Not a wide braking plough; while the skis can be quite far apart, they should only form a shallow angle. The aim is to apply pressure against the edge. To pressure the ski, sink down over the ball of the foot. To edge it, move the thigh inwards with the same action as a snowplough traverse:

1. Set off in a fairly fast gliding plough.
2. Press strongly against the inside edge of one ski and hold it for a moment, then do the same on the other ski.

Don't actually try to turn the skis. While foot steering is normally an important element, the aim here is to apply pure edge pressure without any foot turning. Aim to go in a straight line as you pressure the edge, and see what happens. While the result certainly is a turn, it's the skis which are turning you rather than the other way round. It feels as if they are on rails, travelling round a fast, curving track.

One way to visualize the action is to imagine there's a spring connected

Fig 78 (a) and (b)   The racing snowplough. Instead of turning your feet, simply press strongly against the edge of the ski. As a result, the ski carries you around a fast, carved track.

(a)

(b)

between your hip and your hand. Stretch the spring each time you turn:

Travelling downhill in a plough, stretch one

spring as far as you can and hold it for a moment. Stretch it from both ends at once – pull inwards with your hip while reaching out and downwards with your hand.

The 'spring-stretching' action creates angulation. It encourages leg-lean (by pulling inwards with the hip) and foot pressure (by reaching out and downwards with the hand). You can also use it to gain feedback about your skiing:

Check the stiffness of each imaginary spring as you turn. If they feel very stiff, imagine they're elastic bands instead. Now check how symmetrical they are. Do they both stretch by the same amount, or is one softer than the other?

Even out any variation in stiffness. Then, having practised in a plough, try it with skis parallel. Use a slow tempo to give time to feel what is happening.

Starting the Carve

This spring-stretching action provides control during the main arc of the turn. The other key to effective carving is the initiation. Too much foot turning causes

Fig 79   'Stretching the spring'. Imagine there's a spring connecting your outer hip and hand. Whether ploughing or parallel, you can create powerful edge grip by stretching the spring. Make sure to pull equally from both ends at once.

Fig 80 (a)–(c)   To create strong edge-pressure at the start of the turn, push down against the top ski by extending the leg. Rather than pushing the ski out sideways to produce a stem, aim to push it directly downwards into the snow.

(c)

(b)

skidding. Instead, the turns must also be started with edge-pressure.

One approach is to use leg extension. The action was first described in Chapter 5 under 'Plough Pumping'. From a flexed, angulated position at the end of the previous turn, push down against the top ski to initiate the new one. Rather than pushing the ski out to the side (which deflects it into a stem), push down perpendicularly against the snow:

Imagine you're skiing on foam rubber. To initiate each turn, push the new outer ski down into the surface.

To give the skis time to respond, stretch out the turns (see Chapter 7). It gives a smoother initiation, and reduces the tendency to foot-turn. At the start, the outer ski must be edged as well as pressured. Provided your body follows its flow-line across the path of the skis, they will automatically roll onto the new edges. As before, the leg extension projects you downhill.

Fig 81   Giles Green in action in a steep couloir.

Step Turning

Another way to initiate a carve is by stepping onto the new outer ski. It's a racing technique, but is also an excellent way for non-racers to develop dynamic and positive leg action:

1. Towards the end of the old turn, step your uphill ski 10–20cm out to the side.
2. To start the new turn, simply lift the downhill ski off the snow, transferring all your weight onto the uphill one.

As well as transferring pressure onto the new outer ski, the step projects your body into the turn. Instead of your body 'falling' downhill across the skis, the step displaces your skis uphill of your body. Lifting the downhill ski removes the leg which was supporting you. That lets your body incline into the turn, and simultaneously applies pressure to the new outer ski.

There are actually three different types of step turn: stem step, parallel step and scissors or skating step. Each has a specific racing application. The parallel step is the most general purpose of the three, with the ski remaining parallel to its partner

(a)

(a)

(b)

Fig 82 (a)–(e)   The parallel step turn.

Fig 82 (a)–(e)   By stepping onto the new outer ski, positive pressure is applied to it at the very start of the turn. If the ski is stepped a small way out to the side, the body automatically inclines into the new turn as the other ski is lifted off the snow.

during the step, and initially being placed flat on the snow. In the stem step (generally used for quick, tight turns in slalom), the ski is stepped onto its inside (big toe) edge. As the name suggests, it's normally also stemmed out at an angle.

The scissors step is used for the wide, sweeping turns of giant slalom, super-G and downhill. The step is made onto the outer (little toe) edge, so that the current turn continues on the uphill ski. Only after the ski is rolled onto its inside edge does the new turn begin.

Fig 83   The stem step.

Fig 84   The scissors or skating step.

(c)

(d)

(e)

Fig 85 (a)–(e)   Illustrated here in parallel form, the skier rebounds powerfully from foot to foot, creating tightly linked turns with minimum skid.

Short-Radius Carving

To carve tighter turns, the same racing snowplough can be used, but at a fast tempo so you drop quickly onto the edge. Instead of staying low while the skis continue round a longer turn, rebound immediately upwards, so you bounce quickly from edge to edge. Use the springy resilience of your boots to help provide the rebound:

Set off in a shallow plough, and spring powerfully from foot to foot. Imagine the rhythm of a ball bouncing downhill, with no pause or break in the tempo.

The previous turns were long, smooth carves; this time the action creates much shorter, snappier turns. The sudden pressure bends the ski strongly into reverse camber. The rebound immediately releases the pressure again, transferring it to the new ski. As the ski comes out of reverse camber, it automatically springs parallel to its neighbour. The more strongly it grips and bends, the more positive the effect. But if you pause before starting the new turn, that spring energy is lost and the plough remains.

It's analogous to using a bow and arrow. If you pull back the bow and release it, the arrow flies true, but if you reduce the tension again before release, the arrow simply drops at your feet. Pausing between turns loses the ski's spring energy, so you shoot yourself in the foot.

Shortswing

The same quick, snappy edge pressure is used in another manoeuvre known as shortswing. Although it's not a carved turn, it has many features in common with short-radius carving. By turning your feet as you rebound off the edges, the skis pivot across your direction of travel into a skid. By dropping hard against the new

(c)

(d)

(b)

Fig 85 (a)–(e)   Short radius carving.

(a)

(e)

edges, the sudden increase in resistance produces what is called a check or edge-set. Because they're turned across your direction of travel, the skis no longer deflect along their edges in a carve. Instead, the edge-bite opposes the skid, momentarily stopping the skis' sideways motion.

While carving maximizes your speed, the skid-check of shortswing gives very slow, tight turns. Skidding provides the speed control; the check gives a strong initiation to the new turn. By halting the skid, the check bends the skis strongly into reverse camber. That bending gives a powerful rebound into the new turn. It provides energy which must otherwise come from your muscles, increasing the efficiency of the turns.

To work effectively, a good pole-plant is also vital. It anchors your upper body, allowing your legs and feet to pivot without disturbing balance or control. The timing of the pole-plant must be precise, occurring just as the skis rebound from the check. As your hips drop down into the check, the pole comes down into the snow. Reinforce the timing by saying 'Check!' with each edge-set and pole-plant.

KEY POINT

While shortswing requires positive foot-turning, the vertical rebound off the edge-set is also very important. A common fault is to put too much emphasis on turning the skis, and too little on the upwards unweighting action.

With an effective edge-set and pole-plant, the rebound not only helps unweight the skis, it also pivots them into the new turn. Provided the upper body is anchored while facing downhill, the legs and feet uncoil powerfully underneath.

Rather than trying to turn the skis quickly, aim to spring them right off the snow so they can pivot freely. By concentrating on the vertical movements, the foot turning takes very little effort.

Fig 86   Opposite: Jean Zimmer and Wayne Watson.

Fig 87 (a)–(c)   Shortswing.

Fig 87 (a)–(c)   With a strong upwards bounce, the skis are pivoted across the direction of travel to create a skid. By dropping down hard against the edges, the resulting check or edge-set gives a positive rebound into the following turn.

(a)

(b)

(c)

Fig 88 (a)–(e)   The serpentine carve.

(a)

Fig 88 (a)–(e)   By flexing the legs to absorb the pressure build-up at the end of the turn, and then extending out against the new edges, the skier's body remains at a near-constant level throughout the turns.

(b)

(c)

(e)

(d)

The Serpentine Carve

The essence of carving lies in bending the ski into the appropriate arc. In long turns, the g-force created by your inertia is usually sufficient once the turn has started. In short turns, the extra force of your body-weight dropping onto the ski provides increased pressure, creating a tighter arc. However, to maintain a precise carve, the amount of pressure must be accurately modulated. In Chapter 7, the forces during the turn were examined. These are less at the start than towards the end of the turn. As a result, either the turn tends to become tighter as it progresses, or else the skis progressively skid.

For a constant, rounded arc, additional pressure must be applied early in the turn, while in the later part it must be reduced. The most effective solution is to use leg extension and flexion. Extending the outer leg to put pressure on the ski has already been dealt with. The new element is to use leg flexion to absorb some of the pressure build-up later in the turn. So far, you've been sinking down to create increased angulation towards the end of the turn; here, the aim is to use a similar action to absorb pressure:

1. To begin with, focus on the pressure against your feet. The aim is to keep it as constant as possible right through turns.
2. As soon as you feel any reduction in pressure, extend your legs to compensate; whenever it increases, pull your feet in towards your body to absorb it.

Instead of your body moving up and down during the turns, it now remains at a near-constant level. In Chapter 4, strength-method ploughing was introduced. There, the hips stayed at a constant height while the plough angle was varied with leg extension and flexion. Here, the sensation is much the same, but instead of pushing out into a plough, both legs are extended to the same side. As the skis sweep beyond your flow-line, the legs extend to maintain the pressure; as the skis cross back underneath your body, the legs bend to absorb the build-up which otherwise occurs.

In tight turns, your body flows straight downhill, while your legs and feet extend rhythmically from side to side. The turns which result are smooth and serpentine, with constant contact between ski and snow the whole way round. The action not only creates carved turns on smooth terrain, it also forms the basis of absorbing bumps. Once more, the mechanical principles of the technique must be matched by a high level of sensitivity when putting them into effect.

PART 4
TACTICS AND TERRAIN

CHAPTER 9

BUMPS

Making Moguls

There are some conditions that lull you into a false sense of security. For example, snow that looks smooth and predictable, but which has the consistency of wet cement or boilerplate. However, there are others which scare you to death just looking at them. Bumps – or moguls – tend to fall into the second category. But their bark is often worse than their bite. The biggest problem is just making sense of them. At first sight, a bumps field has a haphazard appearance, a random array of obstacles strewn down the hillside. However, bumps do actually follow a pattern. Not a very regular one to be sure, but then nor are the slopes on which they are found. The first step towards making sense of them is to understand how they are formed.

Think back to the ideas of flow and resist, and to the pressure against your legs and feet as you turn. Neither resistance nor pressure remain constant. They vary throughout each turn, reaching a maximum towards the end. The skis therefore press into the snow most strongly towards the end of each turn. That creates grooves or troughs in the snow which are deepest near the end of the turn and shallowest at the start. While a single skier barely leaves a trace on firm snow, twenty would leave a clearly defined trough if they followed the same route.

It's most obvious in either of two situations: on a slalom course, where even in icy conditions a rut forms after only a few racers; and in fresh snow, where each skier's tracks can be clearly seen.

Skiers seldom follow exactly the same route. But the terrain determines the best places to turn – you slow down before difficult sections, and start your turns on convex rather than concave areas.

Troughs start forming near these features. Once started, they spread both up and downhill of their source. Up, because the troughs themselves create new obstacles; down, because one turn influences where the next one will start. The result is as if an array of slalom courses had been set side-by-side across the slope, so the ruts became interlinked; or as if several dozen experts had skied a field of powder snow, leaving interlaced, figure-eighted tracks.

Bumps don't get built up; rather, the troughs are cut downwards. The bumps are what remains of the original surface, while the troughs reflect the skiers' routes downhill. To begin with, you're not going to take that line; especially in large bumps, it's faster and more difficult to follow. However, once you have developed your confidence and technique, it's one of the routes which you can choose.

Looking for a Line

The first task is reading the terrain – picking a line through the bumps. Provided it's not too difficult – not too steep or icy, nor the bumps themselves too big – then skiers of any standard can (and indeed often must) learn to cope. Within these limitations, technique is less important than the ability to choose a good line. Even snowplough skiers can learn to negotiate gentle bumps, and indeed come to enjoy it.

Focusing Attention

The biggest single barrier is fear. How you direct your attention has a strong bearing on how intimidating a slope looks. If you take a wide-angle view, you're much more likely to be overawed than if you look at a small area. Focus on one turn at a

Fig 89   Bumps are what remains of the original surface, after the passage of many skiers has eroded the surrounding snow.

(a)

(b)

Fig 90 (a)–(c) By initiating your turns on the crests of the bumps, only the mid-section of the skis is in contact with the snow. As a result, the turns start very easily. To help get the timing right, aim to plant your pole on the crest of the bump.

(c)

time. Look for where to make your next turn, not ten or twenty turns ahead. Nor do you need to look at the bumps on either side of your line – only at the snaking corridor down which you're going. Not only does a narrow focus reduce anxiety, it also helps you pick your line. A wide-angle view gives too much information.

Using the Crests

The shorter the ski, the easier it turns.

KEY POINT

To help follow a line over the crests, focus on your pole-plant. See how accurately you can plant it, aiming for top dead centre of each bump. It also helps you to keep turning, and to avoid those 'Will I, won't I?' traverses across the slope.

That's why beginners use small skis. On a bump, only the part of the ski directly beneath your foot touches the snow. Momentarily, you're on a very short ski. At that point, the tip and tail are completely clear of the surface. On the other hand, in the troughs the extremities press firmly against the snow, making the skis grip strongly. It's therefore easiest to initiate your turns on the crests. At that point you may be on less than 30cm of ski. Turning a ski of that length is easy.

The fact that bumps make turning easy can help reduce anxiety. Instead of seeing them as hazards – as obstacles to be avoided – view them as opportunities, as features that help you turn:

Set off down a gentle bumps run, and aim for the biggest, most convex ones. Don't zigzag wildly in search of them, just choose a smooth route that takes in the biggest bumps.

Focusing on a positive goal ('Where's the next big bump?') can dissolve the negative thoughts ('Oh God, these bumps are huge!').

The aim is not, however, to pivot sharply on the bumps. The turns should be smooth Ss rather than jerky Zs. From the crest, turn down the face of the bump into the trough. There, the concave shape provides extra grip to finish the turn.

Turning too sharply is one of the most common errors. Despite the help which they give, bumps are more intimidating than smooth terrain. There's a great temptation to turn quickly, to spend the minimum time travelling – or looking – steeply downhill. That tendency is increased by focusing solely on the crests. While it initially helps you pick a line, it also blocks your awareness of other important terrain features. In particular, you may fail to notice how much distance there is between the bumps. That's the space you have for turning in. So now, switch focus onto the gaps between the bumps: do the turns extend from one bump to the next, or do they finish sooner? If necessary, stretch them out.

Turning too quickly causes excess skid. As a result, you slither sideways down the face of the bump and come to a sudden stop when you hit the trough. That jars your legs and disrupts balance. With rounder turns, the skis grip more firmly. While skidding is necessary for speed control, it should be in an arc rather than sideways downhill.

Acceleration and Deceleration

The principle of initiating your turns on the crests and finishing them in the troughs can be applied to any convex and concave areas to make turning easier. One consequence is that while convex terrain gets progressively steeper, concave terrain gets shallower. So the slope contours accentuate the skis' tendency to accelerate in the first half of the turn and decelerate in the second.

From the crest of each bump, the terrain drops away more steeply than the slope's overall gradient, while in the trough it becomes gentler. The effect is to disrupt your balance. The acceleration tends to make you overbalance backwards; as you enter the trough, the deceleration pitches you forwards again.

Fig 91 (a)–(c)   When linking your turns down the fall-line, make sure your upper body keeps facing in the direction of its momentum, i.e. straight downhill.

(a)

(b)

(c)

Body Forwards

You've already used projection to deal with acceleration. In bumps it's even more important, but because of the temptation to turn quickly, it's essential to make sure that your body doesn't rotate as you do it. If your body rotates, you simply fall into the hill. Instead of your centre of mass following its flow-line across the path of your skis, rotation throws you towards the centre of the turn.

1. Check the orientation of your shoulders and hips. Are you facing downhill of your skis, or swinging your body round into the hill? Focus on facing along your line of momentum.
2. Pick a target directly downhill, and keep your torso facing towards it. Use the goalkeeper and belly-button spotlight exercises to help stabilize your shoulders and hips.

On smooth terrain you can use an up-forward movement to initiate your turns. But unless you're going very slowly, it makes you take off from the tops of the bumps. Especially if you lack confidence, there's a strong temptation to use this bunny-hop action to turn quickly. However, that encourages excess skid, the consequences of which you've already seen. Instead, relax the outside leg at the end of the turn. On smooth terrain, it

transfers pressure to the new outer ski and allows your body to follow its flow-line. Here it also helps absorb some of the upwards throw of the bump itself.

Feet Forwards

The extra acceleration into the turns is matched by a stronger deceleration in the second half. Unless you compensate, it pitches you forwards and downhill before starting the next turn. To accommodate the deceleration, you must shift your balance slightly further back during the second half of the turn. As your skis cross the fall-line, gently push both feet forwards so that they move ahead of your hips. It's not a matter of sitting back. Far from being a static position, it's a dynamic movement that constantly adjusts your point of balance.

As the turn starts, your momentum flows forward and downhill, shifting the pressure onto the balls of your feet. Then, as the skis approach the fall-line, you must shift the pressure back over your heels, ready for the ensuing deceleration which will help project your body forwards again into the start of the new turn.

Indoor Exercise

You can get the feel of this feet-forward action while sitting in an upright chair. Sit with your feet resting lightly on the floor, and slide them gently forward and back. Provided your feet remain flat on the floor, the movement comes from the knees and ankles. Your shins pendulum back and forth, hinging from the knees. Wearing skis, your feet can't slide so far forward, since the boots prevent your ankles extending past the vertical.

The movement comes from ankles and knees rather than higher up the body. If you push your hips forwards as well, your torso ends up leaning back, upsetting your balance. Provided you're in a flexed 'goalkeeper' stance, you can push both feet forward without disturbing your balance, since the boots stop your feet moving too far ahead. Try the action while traversing across a gentle slope:

1. Set off at a shallow angle in a flexed stance.

Fig 92 (a)–(c)   The 'foot forward' action for shifting pressure along the ski. In a traverse, shoot both feet forward, then drive your shins forward to resume your original stance.

(c)   (b)   (a)

2. Shoot both feet forwards, then push your shins forwards to regain your original stance.

3. Repeat the action rhythmically as you continue across the traverse.

The entire movement comes from below the hips. If the upper body moves too, you'll lose your 'goalkeeper' stance. It's quite an odd sensation, as your legs and feet pendulum back and forth beneath you. Your point of balance shifts between the balls of your feet and your heels, but without making you overbalance.

Once you've practised the action in a traverse, try it while turning. At first, do it on smooth terrain:

Drive both shins forwards to initiate the turns, then gently push your feet through in the second half.

As with most other movements in skiing, it should be smooth and continuous rather than sudden and jerky. Match the tempo to the turns, so the movement extends through their entire duration. It has several effects. Driving your shins forward increases the pressure on the front of the skis, giving a positive initiation. It links neatly with the projection of your upper body: as the torso 'falls' downhill into the new turn, the shins push forwards in the same direction. Then, in the second half, the feet-forward action shifts pressure towards the tails of the skis. That helps stretch out the turn, and prepares you for the skis' deceleration. The next step is to try it in bumps:

From a flexed posture, smoothly push your feet forwards into the trough during the second half of the turn. As the resistance builds up, it tends to push your feet back underneath you again as you start the new turn.

The action must be matched to the terrain, the timing and extent following the contours of the snow. It requires both sensitivity to the skis, and accurate reading of the terrain. In bumps more than anywhere else, your point of balance shifts along the entire length of your foot,

sometimes forward over the ball of the foot, sometimes right back on your heel.

This foot-forward/shin-forward action makes it feel as if your feet and skis are shifting back and forth beneath you, while your body remains stable over the top. However, if the actions aren't geared to the terrain, the sensation is rather that your body is pitching back and forth above the skis, sometimes leaning back, sometimes hanging forwards.

Absorption and Pressure Control

Bumps amplify the pressure changes against your skis. As you come through the troughs the pressure increases; going over the crests, it drops away and tends to throw you into the air. Unless you compensate, that severely limits your control.

The Human Suspension System

Fortunately, human beings have got the most sophisticated suspension system in the world – a very powerful computer connecting your legs to your eyes. If engineers could match it, Formula One cars

could race on country lanes. Two features make our suspension system so special.

First is the range of travel. Lifting your knee as high as possible towards your chest raises your foot 50–75cm clear of the ground. That's your suspension's vertical range. It's about twice that of the best moto-cross bike, and they're among the most effective vehicles for rough terrain. In fact, moto-cross riders use their legs in exactly the same way as bumps skiers, to cope with large undulations.

The second feature is the ability to anticipate what's coming. A car's wheel must hit the bump before the suspension reacts. The pressure pushes the wheel up against the spring, while the car stays at about the same level. But you can anticipate the bump, and start pulling your feet up before the pressure increases. On reaching the drop-off on the other side, extend your legs to maintain contact.

The aim is to be one step ahead of the car. Its suspension responds to pressure changes, absorbing undulations without affecting the vehicle. Skiers can eliminate the pressure variations themselves. As your legs pump up and down, they follow the contours of the terrain. By anticipating the bumps rather than just reacting to them, you can maintain constant pressure beneath your feet.

Fig 93 (a)–(c) Absorbing bumps on a traverse.

Fig 93 (a)–(c) Notice how the skier's head remains at exactly the same level against the skyline, while the legs flex and extend to absorb the bump.

(a)

The technique is called compression or absorption. In French, it's called 'avalement' (swallowing); in German, 'Wellen' (waves); in Italian, 'absorbimento'. Whatever the name, the principle remains the same. While the skis go up and down over the bumps, your body remains undisturbed.

Learning to Absorb

Your body must be loose and relaxed in bumps. You can't develop the technique if the range of movement lies outside your 'comfort zone'. Start with some exercises to develop your mobility. Do them while schussing down a smooth, easy slope:

1. Lift alternate knees close to your chest.
2. Jump both skis high off the snow and land softly.
3. Bend and stretch over as big a range as possible.

It's best to start learning to absorb while traversing through bumps. As well as requiring a bigger range of movement than normal, the actions must be co-ordinated with the terrain before you try turning:

1. Pick a gentle line which goes over some fairly large bumps.

2. Before setting off, find a point of reference at the far end of your traverse.
3. Imagine a straight line running between your eyes and that point. Keep your eyes on the line the whole time. While your legs pump up and down over the bumps, your head remains still and level.

You can also pretend that the top of your head is just touching an imaginary ceiling. All the way across, keep your head brushing against the ceiling.

Another exercise is to imagine you're balancing a book on your head. Keep it balanced the whole time. If you succeed with this, try a brim-full glass of schnapps.

You can keep your head level in one of two ways – by folding and extending your legs while the upper body remains still, or by dipping and straightening your torso as well. In bumps, the aim is to keep your torso as still as possible, maintaining a dynamic, balanced posture but without jack-knifing from the waist each time you hit a bump. That's helped by focusing on what your centre of mass is doing:

Traverse towards a reference point, and visualize a line running from it to your navel. Keep your navel on the line all the way across.

You can also use the belly-button spotlight exercise. Instead of shining the spotlight straight downhill, keep it focused on the reference point:

While your legs fold and extend over the bumps, keep the spotlight level as it shines on your target.

Having developed the basic movements, try anticipating the bumps to maintain constant pressure between skis and snow. It's simply a refinement of the action, and has a similar objective to the serpentine carve described in Chapter 8. Focus on the pressure through your legs and feet. While your point of balance moves back and forth, the total pressure stays constant:

1. As the skis rise up the face of a bump, absorb the pressure build-up.
2. As they come over the crest, push your feet down to maintain contact.

Sometimes the trough isn't preceded by a bump. Because there's nothing to compress your legs, you must sink down in anticipation of the extension. It's like squatting down before jumping off a high wall, so that you don't have so far to drop. Always look ahead, to anticipate and prepare. When driving a car, you change

(b)

(c)

(a)

(b)

(c)

(d)

Fig 95 (a)–(d) Absorption while turning over the crest of a bump.

Fig 95 (a)–(d) Note the pole-plant on the crest of the bump for accurate timing. Once more, the skier's head remains at about the same level, while the legs fold to absorb the bump then extend into the trough.

down before rather than when you need the extra power; you move your hands round the wheel before reaching a corner, ready to turn it.

'Sitting Back' in Bumps

In Fig 93, the point of contact moves along the ski over a large range. It can momentarily end up behind your heels, just before the skis drop into the hollow. As a result, you'll sometimes feel that you're sitting back when absorbing large bumps. It's also due to the limited ankle flex of ski boots, which forces your feet up in front of rather than beneath your hips. It's not 'sitting back' in a static, weight-on-heels sense, any more than in the case of a trampolinist doing a tuck-jump; rather, it's the end-point of a movement.

Folding into a tuck brings the feet in front of the hips for that moment, but as the legs unfold once more, the feet drop back down underneath. You simply need to maintain an athletic stance for good dynamic balance. It links neatly with accommodating the skis' acceleration and deceleration. The feet-forward/knee-forward principle was developed for maintaining balance. In folding to absorb a bump, your point of balance shifts back just as the skis start to decelerate when rising up its face.

Fig 94 Opposite: The Solaise bumps, Val d'Isère.

Absorbing and Turning

The next step is to absorb while turning. As before, the turn starts on the crest and continues into the following trough. At the same time, your legs fold and extend to give your upper body a smooth ride. The trouble is that this involves doing two things at once. Moreover, the vertical movements are the precise opposite of normal. Till now, turns have started with leg extension and finished with a down-sink. By contrast, you're now folding your legs as the turn starts and extending in the second half. To avoid confusion, your approach to the task is important.

By concentrating on the movements themselves – 'Bend my legs to start the turn, extend them to finish' – you're more likely to have problems than if you focus on the task of keeping your body level. Use the same exercises as before:

1. Pick a reference point and keep your head, then your navel, travelling towards it as you turn.

2. Imagine you are balancing something on your head as you ski through the bumps.
3. Monitor the pressure beneath your feet, and keep it as constant as possible through the turns.

The action of absorption has a much bigger range than in normal up-movement turns. That in itself helps reduce the interference. Because it feels different, you are less likely to get the two confused. It's therefore important to develop a good range of movement. Exaggerate the action, even when the bumps are small. It prepares you for bigger ones, and helps ingrain the new movement pattern.

Another feature which reduces confusion is that in up-movement turns, your body rises as the turn starts, then sinks down towards the end. Here, your centre of mass stays at a constant level, while only your legs move up and down.

Fig 96 (a)–(f)
Skiing the trough.

Fig 96 (a)–(f)   This is a much faster line, as indicated by the snow thrown up by the skis. For timing. the pole-plant is on the uphill face of the bump. The head and body remain fairly level, while the legs absorb the undulations in the terrain.

(a)

(b)

(c)

Different Lines

So far your line has gone over the crests of the bumps. But that isn't the line that formed the bumps in the first place. Rather, they're caused by skiers following the troughs. That's a much faster route which stays closer to the fall-line, shown as route A in Fig 99. Following it requires good absorption, to maintain ski-to-snow contact.

In fact there's a trade-off between the degree of undulation and the speed of the line. Going over the crests involves the biggest undulations, but lets you travel fairly slowly. Following the troughs gives more speed but less undulation. However, you actually need just as much absorption on this line as going over the crests. That's because you're not just absorbing the undulations, but the pressure variations as well. Although there's less bump to absorb, you hit it at a higher speed. Unless you absorb it effectively, the impact throws you into the air.

While it's the same action, it feels different at higher speeds. Instead of a smooth bend-and-turn, stretch-and-turn, it becomes a much snappier tuck-kick, tuck-kick. Your legs

---

KEY POINT

To follow the line through the troughs, the pole-plant is again very useful. Plant it on the uphill side of each bump, directly behind the crest. Once more, by focusing on planting on the back of every bump you come to, you're much more likely to maintain the rhythm of turning.

To ski the trough, you must also turn with minimum skid. The trough is like an undulating bobsleigh track: there's very little room for turning the skis diagonally to your direction of travel. The key elements are pressure control and edging; using absorption to maintain pressure against the skis, and edging strongly for grip. Too much foot turning makes the tails catch on the bumps.

(d)

(e)

(f)

Fig 97 (a)–(c)   Getting airborne. This should only be practised where there's a safe landing and run-out. Apart from developing balance and confidence when in the air, it's also a useful way of avoiding unexpected obstacles.

(c)   (b)   (a)

bend rapidly on hitting the bump, folding into a tucked position. As you come over the highest point, you must snap your feet quickly down again to maintain contact. Sometimes it's impossible to stay in contact. If the terrain drops away faster than you can extend your legs, you inevitably get airborne. But even in this situation you should still *aim* to keep your skis on the snow.

Speed Control in the Fall Line

At higher speeds, you're absorbing the impact of ski against snow as much as the contours of the terrain. That absorption provides additional speed control. It's a similar principle to checking. The impact transfers some of your momentum to the ground, slowing you down by an equivalent amount.

With the skis at an angle to your direction of travel, they can easily provide resistance, either gradually through skidding, or suddenly through checking. However, when skiing the troughs down a bumps field, the skis stay close to the fall-line, and to your direction of travel.

To understand how you can check in

Fig 98 (a) and (b)   Each time the skis hit a bump, momentum is transferred to the ground.

KEY POINT

It's useful to practise getting airborne, so when it happens you're better able to keep control. Choose a small bump on its own, or the last one in a series. It should have a smooth landing and safe run-out:

1.   From a short run-up, let the bump push you into the air. On landing, bend deeply to absorb the impact.
2.   Within your limits of confidence, gradually increase your run-up speed.
3.   From a slower run-up, push off as you go over the bump. Instead of just letting it throw you, extend your legs to get more height.

You can also jump to avoid particularly deep or nasty ruts, landing on the far side. You need excellent timing and judgement, even in the easiest of bumps, but it's a useful technique for avoiding a solitary rut, or even an exposed rock or other obstacle.

that situation, you need to consider what's happening in the third dimension. If you don't absorb a bump, it throws you into the air. Your speed downhill is reduced by just the amount with which you are deflected upwards. In other words, the impact with the crest of the bump has a slowing-down effect. In a check, the skis have to be across your flow-line, but when hitting a bump, you slow down even with your skis pointing straight downhill. However, it's only a temporary effect. After going up in the air, gravity accelerates you downwards again.

Instead, you must absorb the upward force. If you don't, the bump throws your entire body upwards. But by absorbing the impact, only your feet and legs get pushed up. Your muscles act as shock-absorbers, preventing your centre of mass from being deflected. Therefore, each time your legs absorb the impact with a bump, it slows you down a little. It's like running downhill – each time your heel strikes the surface, momentum is transferred to the ground.

When running, you also must absorb the reaction force, resisting with your leg muscles as your body tries to continue downhill. If you don't absorb, you spring upwards in a great bounding stride, with little loss of speed. The faster you're running or the steeper the slope, the harder it is to slow down. You can feel the effort in your thigh muscles each time your foot strikes the ground. In skiing, the sensations are very similar, except that both legs absorb in unison instead of one at a time.

Expert bumps skiers often keep their skis very close to the fall-line. Yet they still travel much slower than if they schussed down the same gradient with no bumps. The bigger the bumps, the more they slow you down. On a smooth slope, you can't create any resistance without turning your skis. But the deeper the troughs are cut into the snow, the greater the impact and the more momentum that can be transferred.

Unfriendly Bumps

Large bumps can develop pronounced drop-offs, especially on steep slopes. They sometimes become undercut, with sheer faces on their downhill sides. No matter how good your technique, some of them are just downright unpleasant. You fall off them rather than ski over them. These 'square-edged' bumps often result from

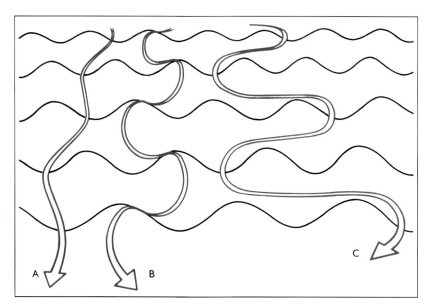

Fig 99   Different lines.
   Line A: following the trough. This is the fastest, most direct route.
   Line B: skiing the crests. By deviating further from the fall-line and allowing the skis to skid down the faces of the bumps, a much slower descent is possible.
   Line C: skiing a slow route through the trough. Where the bumps have awkward shapes and drop-offs, this line allows speed control while avoiding the bumps themselves.

skiers traversing across the hillside rather than skiing down it. Traversing cuts into the downhill face of the bumps. The more nervous the skier, the more they turn uphill to follow a shallow line. As a result, their skis turn into the bumps, eroding them still further.

A key point is to avoid being one of those skiers. Trying to ski bumps that are too difficult not only spoils your fun, it ruins it for others too, wrecking what could otherwise have been a good mogulfield. Sometimes it's unavoidable, but whenever possible, choose slopes that are within your ability – ones that are challenging, but where you can still make linked turns.

But what can you do when the bumps have these awful shapes? Going over the crests doesn't work, because instead of skiing smoothly down the face of the bump, you just fall off the edge. By following the trough, you pick up too much speed. The answer is to find a

different line. For speed control you still must turn a long way from the fall-line. The best route is to follow the troughs right around each bump rather than snaking down between them.

This is shown as route C in Fig 99. It deviates even further from the fall-line than the route going over the crests, but because the trough gives less room for skidding, you need the extra amount of turning to control your speed. It's important to make smooth, rounded turns. If you turn too sharply, the skis plough into the side of the bump instead of following the trough. However, because the terrain is intimidating, that's often hard to avoid.

The best solution is by focusing your attention. Actively seek out a line that curves around the bumps, and follow it as accurately as you can. Don't look too far ahead – one or two turns is plenty. Instead, use your visual imagination to make the track stand out as clearly as possible.

CHAPTER 10

SKIING DEEP SNOW

It's one of skiing's most appealing and enviable images – bright pastel figures leaving curving vapour-trails of powder as they swoop down the mountainside. Symmetrical, sinuous tracks left in the fresh snow as a testimony to their skill, while they float effortlessly from turn to turn. Back in the real world, many skiers face a rather different experience. More often it's a rising tide of frustration and exhaustion as they flounder in the soft, enveloping folds. Or perhaps just straightforward exhaustion, having excavated the equivalent of a large car-park in search of a missing ski. The first experience of deep snow or off-piste can be extremely disheartening. But why does it feel so different – and so much more difficult – than other snow conditions?

Fig 100   Powder skiing.

The Medium

Firstly, your skis are *in* rather than on the snow. Even on prepared runs, your skis sometimes sink into the surface – for example, on loosely packed powder or wet spring snow. While these conditions are more difficult than hardpack, the problems become even greater in deep snow. When both skis disappear beneath the surface, the difficulties are both technical and psychological.

Technically, the main problem is that there's more resistance to the skis turning. Because they're surrounded by snow, the skis can't skid sideways so freely. The snow builds up against their sidewalls, making them harder to turn and more prone to catching edges. The increased lateral resistance can make the skis behave as if they were caught in a rut. If they happen to be pointing in different directions, the result is the effective but undignified ostrich stop.

In anything more than a few centimetres of soft snow, the skis can sink to varying depths depending on the pressure on them. That makes balancing harder and increases the chances of the skis crossing, since one can simply slide beneath the other.

The main psychological problem is fear of the unknown. Not only are the skis harder to turn, they also respond differently and unpredictably. If they disappear beneath the surface, you lose all visual reference – are they ploughing, parallel or crossed? which way are they pointing? are they still on your feet? Anxiety and uncertainty cause muscle tension and reduced mobility, restricting your control. Added to the technical difficulties, the outcome is often frustration and failure. To minimize these problems and give the greatest chance of success,

you must carefully select the best conditions for learning.

Avalanche Danger

The overriding consideration is safety. Scores of skiers die or are badly injured each winter due to avalanches – in most cases, triggered by the victims themselves. The only way to eliminate these dangers is never to go skiing in the mountains. Even on-piste, there is a small but ever-present risk. In deep snow, those risks become much greater.

While the dangers are both serious and real, they can be minimized by acting sensibly and with caution. The simplest and safest advice is to ski off-piste only under the guidance of a qualified instructor or mountain guide. That means a professionally qualified 'Guide de Haute

Fig 101   Many skiers are killed in avalanches every year.

difficult to bring the skis parallel again if they go their separate ways.

Make your first attempt at powder skiing in just a light covering of new snow. Between 10 and 20cm is ideal. With less than 10cm there's hardly any difference to skiing on piste; with more than 20cm it's initially quite difficult to turn. In deep snow the skis begin floating as you gain speed. Instead of staying on the firm base layer, they plane upwards through the soft snow. A shift of weight makes one ski sink while the other rises up, disturbing your balance. Also, the deeper the snow, the harder it is to get up from a fall. After going base over apex in a metre of powder, you can look like an octopus in treacle as you struggle to get out.

Montagne', 'Bergführer' or member of the UIAGM (International Union of Mountain Guides). Ski guides employed by tour companies are not in this category.

Detailed advice on snow and avalanche safety are beyond the scope of this book. For those who are interested, see Further Reading on page 127. However, information from books is a poor substitute for the intimate local knowledge and experience of professional guides and instructors. Their advice should always be sought and carefully followed.

As well as ensuring that the snow is stable, it's important also to choose suitable terrain. There are three separate aspects to consider – the snow texture, its depth, and the slope itself. Unless all three are right, first attempts in deep snow almost always end in frustration.

The Right Stuff

Untracked snow comes in a wide variety, from light dry talcum powder – known as 'champagne' in the USA – to heavy and glutinous wet cement, known both in Scotland and abroad as 'porridge'. The first is fine; the second all but impossible.

Light, fluffy snow offers the least

resistance to your skis, so they turn easily and predictably; but if it's wet or heavy, or fell in windy conditions, just walking around on skis is difficult. Once moving downhill, staying in control is even harder. The heavier the snow, the greater its resistance. As noted above, it's like getting your skis caught in a rut. This makes it much harder to recover from mistakes. Even a slight loss of balance makes your skis drift apart or get crossed.

To test the snow texture, make a snowball from it. The less it clings together, the better it is for skiing. The denser and wetter the snow, the more easily it forms a ball.

If you can wring water out of it, go for a Glühwein instead. But if the snow won't form a ball no matter how hard you press, and trickles through your fingers like dry sand, just keep a sharp lookout; you might get hurt in the rush.

The Right Depth

As well as snow texture, depth is also important. The deeper it is, the harder it is to ski. Just as in heavy snow, it's very

The Right Slope

The next decision is what slope to use. Apart from issues of safety, your choice of slope has a strong bearing on ease of learning. There are several aspects to consider.

The first is its shape. Not just the shape you can see now – even more important is what was there before the last snowfall. An icy mogulfield can look quite inviting after a fall of powder, but the bumps are still there, even though they're hidden.

Pick a slope with a smooth, firm base under the fresh snow. Because your skis sink through it, whatever is underneath still affects their behaviour. Ice, bumps and breakable crust should all be avoided when they lie beneath the surface.

Gradient is also important. It's no good if the run is so gentle that your skis hardly move; since fresh snow produces more resistance than hardpack, you'll need a steeper slope than you might at first think. However, one of the biggest problems to begin with is getting the skis to turn at all. The first few attempts usually involve ballistic skiing, i.e. travelling out of control in a straight(ish) line, followed by a spot of digging to extricate all the bits.

Even with the extra resistance of deep snow, you can pick up more speed than you had intended if the slope is too steep. The gradient should be gentle enough to schuss down; if it flattens out at the bottom, you needn't worry about stopping.

The best slope for learning off-piste skiing is actually a well-maintained blue or red run just after a snowfall. It's less likely to avalanche, and should be free of rocks, tree stumps or holes that might trip you or cause injury.

The Kick-Turn

One useful deep snow technique which hasn't been covered is the kick-turn. It's a means of turning round to face the other way when standing still. If you're facing the wrong way, stepping around with a clock turn can be hard work in deep snow. The kick-turn is quicker and takes less effort. It does however require good balance and agility. It should first be mastered on the flat, then practised on firmly pisted snow before trying it off-piste:

1. Put both poles behind you in the snow, with your hands on top of the grips so you can lean on them for support. If you're on a slope, the poles should be uphill of your skis, with your body facing downhill.
2. Kick your downhill ski up on to its tail, and pivot it outwards to bring the tip beside its partner's tail. You're now standing with your skis at 180° to each other. Then step the second ski round parallel, to face the opposite way.

If you lack the flexibility to turn your feet at 180° to each other, you can damage knee ligaments or tear muscles. Doing it

Fig 102 (a)–(c)   To begin with, choose a smooth and gentle slope with only a light covering of fresh snow.

(a)

(b)

(c)

with bent knees increases your range of rotation a little, but if you're still a long way from 180°, it's best not to pursue it. The only way of doing an effective kick-turn in this situation is by springing from one foot to the other. If you skip off the uphill ski before the other one is back on the snow, you don't need so much flexibility. You do, however, need to be very confident and agile.

No matter how flexible or agile you are, always make sure you have a stable platform before starting. In deep snow, stamp down a level area; in icy conditions, make sure your grip is secure; and if it's windy, make sure a gust can't knock you over.

Finally, never do a kick-turn directly above or below another person. It's very easy to misjudge and hit them with your ski, which is especially dangerous with the tip at head height.

The Method

Assuming that the slope is appropriate for learning, the next issue is how you tackle it. Skiing in deep snow is less a matter of learning new techniques, and more of adapting to the altered feel and response.

In the right conditions, any competent parallel skier can master deep snow. There are three key elements:

1. Posture – a relaxed 'goalkeeper' stance, with the legs free to turn independently of the upper body.
2. Flexibility – especially in the ankle joint. If you ski with a stiff lower leg, it's impossible to unweight the skis effectively. Apart from boots that are too stiff, the usual cause is tension in the calf muscles and toes.
3. The ability to turn both skis in unison. While your timing does not have to be perfect, a pronounced stem causes problems. Because of the skis' tendency to track off on their own in deep snow, they're much more likely to catch or get crossed if they don't turn simultaneously.

These three elements represent all the technical tools you need for skiing deep snow. In fact if the snow is very light and shallow, you don't even need that much.

Fig 103 (a)–(c)   The kick-turn.

Fig 103 (a)–(c)   Make sure both poles are firmly planted on the uphill side for support, and that your footing is secure.

(a)

(b)

(c)

Even snowplough skiers can enjoy a few centimetres of fresh powder on a gentle blue.

Setting Off

Whenever you lack confidence, there's a temptation to set off on a gentle traverse to avoid picking up speed, but that makes your first turn much more difficult. The first turn is always the hardest. Starting on a gentle traverse adds to the difficulty, since the skis have got much further to turn. It also prolongs the acceleration phase, so the chances of losing balance are greater.

Instead, set off with your skis pointing straight downhill. That way, the first turn is only a swing to the hill. In effect, it's only half a turn, and the simpler half at that. Because there's no edge change, it's much easier than a complete turn and, having succeeded with the first one, you have much more chance of continuing. Remember too that by rhythmically linking your turns, the skis' natural rebound helps you keep going. That's one reason why gradient is so important; if the slope is too steep, it's much harder to pluck up courage to go for it – to head straight down the fall-line into your first turn.

Finally, avoid following someone else's line. Constantly cutting through other skiers' tracks makes it much harder to maintain control. While ensuring you're in a safe area, always aim for untracked snow.

Taking the Strain

Before setting off, it's tiring to hold yourself in the fall-line. If you lean on the poles, your arms take the strain; if you use a snowplough, it's your legs. Not only is it tiring, it's also harder to relax. In soft snow, you can kick the heels of the skis back into the hillside, forming a level platform to stand on until you set off. You can face downhill for as long as you like, with no strain or tension in your arms or legs:

1. Put your poles behind you as if doing a kick-turn.
2. Lift your lower ski and turn it downhill, then push the tail into the snow beneath

Fig 104 *Setting off. Dig the tails of the skis into the snow as you turn to face downhill. You can then prepare to set off without any strain or muscle-tension.*

your other foot. Dig it in as far as the heel-binding. If necessary slide it back and forth to get it level.
3. Once it's secure, do the same with the other ski.

You can then stand completely relaxed. Get the skis about hip width apart and dead level. From there, you only need a gentle push to get going.

The Bounce

To ski effectively, you must be supple and relaxed. One of the best ways of loosening up is with movement. Before setting off, spend a moment limbering up – jog on the spot, swing your arms and shoulders, make sure your hips and back are loose. Then turn to face downhill ready to go. But before you set off, start to gently bounce up and down. Bend your ankles and knees as deeply as possible to give a soft landing, and bounce at a rhythm that matches the turns that you are going to make:

1. As you start to move, keep on bouncing. Make one or two bounces in the fall-line, then use the next one to initiate your first turn.

2. Continue the rhythm from turn to turn, rebounding upwards from each one into the next.

Here again, the slope's gradient is crucial. If it's too steep, you won't have time to

EQUIPMENT CHECK

For deep snow, your choice of boots and skis is also important. Both should have a soft flex.

On boots with an adjustable flex, set them at their softest. If they have an adjustable forward lean, set them at their most upright. The priority is to have good ankle mobility. But, whatever you do, don't loosen or unclip the tops of your boots – that limits the support, making the ankle much more prone to injury.

The best powder skis have a soft overall flex pattern. Stiff-tailed skis are also satisfactory provided they have a soft forebody (giant slalom skis, for example). The condition of the skis is relatively unimportant in deep snow. You don't need sharp edges, and provided snow doesn't stick to them, the bases can be quite badly gouged without impairing their performance.

Fig 105 (a)–(e)   The Bounce.

(b)

(a)

(c)

Fig 105 (a)–(e) A powerful upward bounce lifts the skis into the lighter uppermost layers of snow, giving an easier start to the turns.

bounce in the fall-line, so you can't establish a rhythm before starting to turn.

The bounce not only helps you stay loose, it also makes turning easier. Fresh snow gets denser with depth, due to the weight pressing down from above. The denser it is, the greater its resistance, making it harder to initiate the turns. Bouncing upwards momentarily reduces the pressure on the skis, letting them rise into the lighter, softer snow to start each turn.

(d)

(e)

Projection

Although deep snow reduces the skis' acceleration, the bounce should still be up-forwards rather than straight up. The forward component helps overcome the tendency to lean back in deep snow, keeping you securely balanced on your skis. As in other situations, the projection is up-forwards with no rotation. If you twist your body, you'll overbalance.

It's the same as in shortswing – use a strong up-movement, and wait for the skis' response before sinking down after the fall-line. Let the skis do the turning; you concentrate on the bounce. If you want to turn more quickly, use a stronger bounce. The more you turn your feet, the more the skis try to skid. While that's fine on hardpack, in powder you'll catch edges and trip.

In deep snow, the turning power comes mainly from edging, not foot steering. Although the skis don't grip the surface as on hardpack, the movements and sensations feel very similar.

The way a ski works in deep snow is rather different from on-piste. While the techniques are similar, the mechanics are not. In deep snow, skis produce 'lift' like a hydrofoil or water-ski. The lift is created by the whole length of the ski, while your weight is concentrated under your foot. The ski therefore bends like an archer's bow, even when going straight. If tilted onto its edge, the shape carries it round a curved path. The more it bends, the tighter the turn. That has three main consequences:

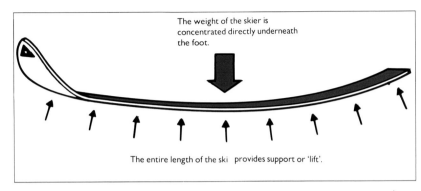

The weight of the skier is concentrated directly underneath the foot.

The entire length of the ski provides support or 'lift'.

Fig 106   In deep snow, the ski is bent into reverse camber even when going in a straight line. Tilted onto an edge, it therefore follows a curving path. The greater the pressure against the ski, the more it bends and the tighter it turns.

1. You must maintain equal pressure on the two skis, otherwise they follow different paths.
2. You must stay relaxed. Control comes from edging rather than foot turning. Your body must be loose enough to angulate effectively.
3. The turn radius is governed by pressure. A stronger bounce creates more pressure against the skis, giving a tighter turn.

You can also use compression turns in deep snow, just as in bumps. The effect is similar to the bounce, lifting the skis into the lighter, uppermost layers to start the turns, while driving them into the denser snow for maximum resistance at the finish. The tightness of turning is governed by the power of the leg extension during the second half of the turn. It's especially effective in dense, heavy snow, as it allows more pressure to be applied, while keeping the upper body quiet and undisturbed.

A Point of Balance

It's sometimes said that you must sit back in deep snow to keep the tips up. But if

(a)

(b)

(c)

Fig 107 (a)–(c)   Compression turns in deep snow. The skier's body remains at a constant level, while the legs fold and extend to control the pressure against the skis. Compare the skier's movements with those of Fig 105.

Fig 108 (a) In deep snow, expert skiers often appear to be sitting back.

Fig 108 (b) Because the skis 'float' tips-high, the skier's centre of mass is actually above the balls of the feet.

STAR TIP

One of the great myths of powder skiing is that you need to lean back. This arises from the illusion that is created by skiers going down a powder slope. On a normal piste the skis would be flat on the snow and at the same angle as the slope. But in deep snow the tips rise to the surface while the tails sink down – hence the skis will be at a less steep angle than the slope.

As you cannot see enough of the skis to appreciate what is happening, it looks as though the skier is leaning back when in fact he is balanced with the weight in the middle of the skis.

Josef Mallaun
Daily Mail Ski Magazine, 1990

you're anxious or out of control, you usually end up sitting back anyway. In deep snow, the difficulty is more often staying far enough forward for balance. Sitting back, your thighs tense up to support your weight. It also reduces the pressure on the front half of the skis. As a result they don't bend as much, which makes them harder to turn.

Instead, stand over the balls of your feet. As your confidence improves and you start skiing faster, you can use the foot-forwards action described in Chapter 9 to deal with the build-up of resistance, but to begin with it's best to stay forward the whole time.

Before setting off, relax your legs and uncurl your toes. Rock forward to get the pressure under the balls of your feet. Then when you set off, stay focused on your legs and feet, keeping them loose and maintaining your point of balance.

If your weight drops back, check your

KEY POINT

Because the bindings are mounted with more ski in front of the boot than behind, skis tend to float tip-high in powder snow even when you're balanced over the balls of your feet. Not only is 'sitting back' an illusion, but the ski tips float high anyway.

hand position. Are you holding a stable hoop? Bringing your hands up or back shifts your balance onto your heels. A positive projection also helps bring you forward over the skis.

Mind Over Matter

With the right slope and snow that's light and not too deep, the biggest remaining problem is psychological. It's largely caused by not being able to see your skis. If you can ignore that and pretend you're on hardpack, the rest is easy. But often, as soon as the skis disappear, you tense up – setting off tentatively instead of committing yourself to the fall-line; trying to force the skis around instead of letting them turn naturally; and leaning back. That's because of what's going on between your ears, not under your feet.

Psychological barriers are among the hardest to overcome. Some general ways of dealing with them were introduced in Chapter 1. Here are some specific exercises to help:

Image and Imagination

A good starting point is to watch powder skiing on video. Go through it several times and imagine yourself doing it as you watch. You can use an instructor's demonstration in the same way. Use your imagination to 'get inside their body' as you watch, to develop a clear idea of what the actions feel like. Then mentally rehearse that image just before setting off. Focus on

Fig 109   Always aim to develop a strong and positive model for your actions.

what the movements should feel like as well as how they look. With a strong model as you set off, there's much more chance of skiing well.

Focused Attention

If you look down at your feet in deep snow, you may panic as soon as the skis disappear. Instead, look ahead towards the spot where you're going to make your next turn. Before setting off, try to visually pin-point where your first turn is going to be. Once

you're moving, keep your line of vision at least one turn ahead of your skis.

Focusing your attention like this can be linked with creating a strong mental image. Before you start, review the first few turns in your mind. Imagine how the movements should feel, and at the same time trace the line you're going to follow with your eyes. Your eyes form the link between imagination and reality, connecting the mental image of *what* you're about to do with *where* it's going to happen on the hillside.

APPENDIX: THE SKI-WAY CODE

The Ski-Way Code is a set of rules drawn up and published by the FIS (the International Ski Federation). They represent a framework for safe and courteous behaviour among skiers. While they don't have the force of law, they are used as the basis for legal action in cases of injury and negligence.

The key points contained in the FIS document are summarized below:

1. Respect others: always act in a manner which doesn't endanger or prejudice others.
2. Ski in control: always adapt your speed and manner of skiing to your personal ability and to the prevailing snow, terrain and weather conditions.
3. Right of way: when coming from above, you must always ensure the safety of those below.
4. Overtaking: always allow a wide margin when overtaking other skiers, so as not to impede their line. It's also important for slower skiers to act predictably, so that anyone who is overtaking can do so safely.
5. Setting off and crossing the piste: whenever you set off, cross, or join a piste, look uphill to avoid skiing out in front of another skier. Then look downhill to avoid running into someone else.
6. Stopping: avoid stopping on a ski run unless it's absolutely necessary. If you must stop, always do so at the edge of the piste, and never where the run narrows, at blind corners and lips, or where there's limited visibility or space. If you fall, move to the side as quickly as possible.
7. Climbing: when climbing uphill, always keep to the edge of the piste. In bad visibility, stay off the piste completely.
8. Obey the signs: always pay attention to warning signs on the mountain. *Never* ski down closed runs or into areas of avalanche danger. As the conventions for piste marking vary from resort to resort, familiarize yourself with the system used. The lift-map usually contains a summary.
9. Assistance at accidents: everyone is duty-bound to assist at an accident. If your help isn't needed, stay out of the way; otherwise stop and do what you can. The ski patrol can be contacted from any café or manned lift station, as well as from emergency telephones located on the slopes.
10. Identification at accidents: if you witness an accident, you must be prepared to give your name and address. If legal proceedings ensue, you may be called on to give evidence.

In addition, three rules of group behaviour might be added:
11. Give all ski groups and classes a wide berth.
12. When stopping, always do so *below* the others in a group, to avoid danger of collision.
13. At the top of ski lifts, move well out of the way before stopping or gathering into a group.

GLOSSARY

Absorption   Using the legs like a car's suspension to iron out bumps in the terrain.

Angulation   Progressive bending at the hips while turning, to provide grip while maintaining balance. Small sideways knee movements are also used to fine-tune the amount of grip.

Anticipation   A downhill facing of the body relative to the skis, as one turn ends and the new one begins. In general, it results from the body facing in the direction of its momentum rather than in the direction the skis are pointing.

Avalement   Using the legs to absorb bumps and control the build-up of pressure against the skis while turning (literally, swallowing).

Ballistic   Used to describe an object which, once in motion, is subject only to external forces, for example, a skier who is unable to control his speed or direction.

Basic swing   An elementary manoeuvre in which the skis are pushed out into a plough to start the turn, then steered parallel to finish it.

Boilerplate   Very hard, icy snow.

Bump   An undulation in the terrain, usually caused by the passage of skiers wearing away the surrounding snow.

Carve   A technique in which the ski turns with minimal skid.

Centrifugal effect   *See* inertia.

Check   A sudden edging of the skis when skidding, which stops or 'checks' the skid. Also known as an edge-set.

Clock turn   A method of turning while stationary by stepping the skis round like the hands on a clock-face. Also known as a star turn.

Compression turn   A similar technique to avalement, used to absorb undulations in the terrain while turning.

Counter-rotation   A technique in which the body is rotated in the opposite direction to that in which the skis are turning.

Crust   A hard, sometimes breakable layer in the snow, produced by the action of sun, wind or a melt-freeze cycle. When created from wind-blown snow, it's known as 'slab' or 'wind-slab'. Not only can it be very difficult to ski, it often poses a serious avalanche risk.

DIN   A standardized scale for binding release settings, from Deutsche Industrie Norm (the German industrial standards institute).

Down unweighting   Unweighting the skis by quickly bending the legs. The term is often misused in reference to the movements of absorption or avalement, in which there's a down movement with no actual unweighting of the skis.

Edge-set   *See* check.

Edging   Tilting a ski onto its edge by leaning the leg sideways. Provided it has pressure on it, the more a ski is edged, the more it tends to grip.

Fall-line   The most direct line down a slope from any given point. Also sometimes referred to as the gravity line.

Flat light   Conditions in which it's difficult or impossible to see the contours of the terrain. It's caused by uniform cloud cover diffusing the sunlight, so that no shadows are cast.

Flow-line   The direction in which a skier's momentum is travelling. When turning, it lies along a tangent to the arc being followed by the skier's centre of mass.

G-force   *See* inertia.

Herringbone   A method of climbing in which the skier faces straight uphill and, keeping the skis at an angle to each other, grips and pushes off against their inside edges.

Inclination   The inward lean of a skier's body, which keeps him or her balanced against the inertial forces generated by turning. Also known as banking.

Inertia   The tendency of a moving object to continue in a straight line. When turning, the skis must grip to overcome inertia and deflect the skier's mass. Inertia is what makes it necessary to lean inwards to maintain balance during a turn. The heavier an object or the faster it moves, the greater its inertia. When turning, the effect of inertia is often referred to as 'the centrifugal effect' or 'g-force'. 'Centrifugal force' is actually a misnomer.

Initiation   The action which starts a turn, for example, pole-planting, stemming, pressure transfer, stepping, unweighting, absorbing, etc.

Kick-turn   A method of turning round while stationary, by lifting one ski onto its tail, pivoting it through 180°, then stepping the other ski around beside it.

Kinaesthesis   The sense of where the body is in space and what it's doing – its orientation, movements and trajectory. The information comes from several sources: touch; vision; the vestibular (balance) organs of the inner ear; specialized receptors in the joints and muscles called proprioceptors.

Mogue   A burrowing alpine mammal found living in colonies beneath mogulfields.

Mogul   *See* bump. Commonly used in the term 'mogulfield', i.e. a run which is covered in bumps.

Off-piste   Any area of hillside which is not officially marked as a run. Off-piste areas contain many more hazards than marked runs, and are not patrolled by the safety and rescue services. The term also refers to deep snow skiing, as in 'off-piste technique'.

PET   An acronym for Pressure-Edge-Turn, which are the three fundamental elements of turning technique.

Piste   A marked and prepared ski run.

Plough   *See* snowplough.

Powder snow   Snow which has fallen in cold, still conditions, giving it a light, fluffy texture.

Pressure   The combination of forces acting on a ski, resulting from the terrain contours, the skier's weight, their body movements, and the inertial forces generated when turning.

Projection   Displacement of the centre of mass forward and downhill at the start of a turn. Although often described as a separate action, it also results from allowing the centre of mass to follow its flow-line at the end of the previous turn.

Schuss   A straight run down the fall-line.

Shortswing   Short-radius turns using a pronounced skid and edge-set, allowing a slow descent down steep, narrow runs.

Side-slipping   Keeping the skis across the fall-line and allowing them to slip sideways. The rate of descent is controlled by the degree of edging.

Side-stepping   A method of climbing in which the skis are kept across the fall-line while stepping sideways.

Skidding   Where a ski is turned at an angle to the direction of the skier's momentum so that it travels more or less sideways. The more the ski is edged, the more resistance is created to oppose its sideways motion.

Skidding to stop   Turning both skis across the direction of travel and skidding to a halt. This is known in North America as a 'hockey stop' (from ice hockey).

Skill   The ability to apply technique in an efficient, versatile and appropriate way.

Snowplough   A technique in which the skis are pushed out at an angle to each other to form an A shape, and used as a means of braking and steering.

Snowplough traverse   A ploughing exercise in which one ski is edged harder while the other is flattened, producing a diagonal crab-like descent.

Spring snow   Snow which has been transformed from feathery snowflakes into coarse, sugar-like crystals (known in North America as 'corn snow'). Since the process of transformation is temperature-related, this type of snow is most common in springtime.

Stemming   Displacing one ski out at an angle to the other, creating an A shape. It's normally used to help initiate a turn. Many parallel skiers use a small stem on difficult terrain, or when lacking confidence.

Step turn   A turn which is initiated by stepping the top (new outer) ski out to the side. The ski may be stepped parallel to its partner, or at a converging (stem step) or diverging (skating or scissors step) angle.

Style   The aspects of movement and posture which embellish technique and differentiate individual and national approaches to skiing. While technique is the functional base, style is the overlay of self-expression.

Swing to the hill   A parallel manoeuvre in which the skis are steered away from the fall-line in a smooth arc.

Technique   The physical actions of skiing (cf. skill above). Technique may be applied in a more or less skilful way. A technique can itself be sound and yet be used inappropriately.

Traversing   Travelling in a straight line across the hill.

Unweighting   Eliminating or reducing the pressure against one or both skis. This is often used as a means of initiating a turn.

Visualization   The re-creation in the imagination of an action previously seen or performed. It can involve modes other than vision, for example, imagining the *feel* of an action as well as picturing its form, and is also known as 'mental imaging'.

White-out   This occurs in conditions of mist or low cloud. Not only do the terrain contours disappear as in flat light, but also the horizon and other points of reference vanish. It is a very disorientating and potentially dangerous situation.

FURTHER READING

General Skiing

Hurn, M. *Skiing Real Snow – the Handbook of Off-Piste Skiing* (The Crowood Press, 1987). The 'Real Snow' of the title refers to snow in its natural, unpisted state. The book contains a wealth of ideas on how to ski it, and on safety and self-rescue for off-piste skiers and ski-tourers. An excellent specialist reference book.

Hurn, M. *Advanced Skiing* (Salamander Books, 1990). A highly readable and beautifully illustrated book which concentrates on advanced-level skiing – fast cruising, bumps and off-piste – as well as looking at the 'Alternative Games' of mono-skiing, snowboarding and telemarking.

Shedden, J. *Skiing: Developing your Skill* (The Crowood Press, 1986). The Director of Coaching of the English Ski Council, John Shedden is one of the leading authorities on skiing. Many of the ideas contained in the foregoing pages were drawn from *Developing your Skill*, which is an excellent book for anyone interested in the processes of learning and teaching.

Shedden, J. *Skilful Skiing* (EP Publishing, 1982). Again this was the source of many ideas used in the foregoing pages. It has the same basic perspective as *Developing your Skill*, but goes more deeply into the (bio)mechanics of the sport. It's highly recommended for anyone seeking an in-depth understanding.

Tejada-Flores, L. *Breakthrough on Skis – How to get Out of the Intermediate Rut* (Random House, 1986). A beautifully simple book on advanced ski technique, written in an easy, informal style. It's hard to find in the UK, but well worth the effort.

Avalanche and Snow Safety

Daffern, T. *Avalanche Safety for Skiers and Climbers* (Diadem Books, 1983). A comprehensive and well-illustrated book on avalanche safety.

Epp, M. and Lee, S. *Avalanche Awareness* (The Wild Side, 1987). Martin Epp is a highly regarded mountain guide, with enormous experience of avalanches and their avoidance.

Fraser, C. *Avalanches and Snow Safety* (John Murray, 1978). Now, unfortunately, it's out of print, but it's still available in libraries. A fascinating book, combining a wealth of readable anecdotes with an in-depth account of modern snow science.

LaChapelle, E. *ABC of Avalanche Safety* (Cordee Press, 1979). A pocket-sized reference on avalanches and their avoidance, written for mountaineers, climbers and skiers.

Ski Fitness

Palmer, S. *Skiing Fit* (The Crowood Press, 1989). An excellent reference covering the full spectrum of training and preparation, for skiers of all levels of ability.

The Mental Side of Skiing

Ferguson, S. *Skiing from the Inside* (Simon & Schuster, 1989). Based on the principles of the 'Inner Game', this book looks at the internal processes which help or hinder our performance as skiers (and indeed as people). A great counterbalance to the many nuts and bolts books on ski technique.

Resort Guides

Gill, C. & Ruck, A. (editors) *Good Skiing Guide* (The Consumer's Association, Hodder & Stoughton). A regularly updated review of ski resorts.

INDEX